Microsoft®

PROJECT 2000

ENI Publishing LTD

500 Chiswick High Road
London W4 5RG

Tel: 020 8956 2320
Fax: 020 8956 2321

e-mail: publishing@ediENI.com
http://www.eni-publishing.com

Editions ENI

BP 32125
44021 NANTES Cedex 1

Tel: (33) 2.51.80.15.15
Fax: (33) 2.51.80.15.16

e-mail: editions@ediENI.com
http://www.editions-eni.com

Straight to the Point collection directed by Corinne HERVO
Translated from the French by Adrienne TOMMY

Foreword

The aim of this book is to let you find rapidly how to perform any task in the project management tool **Project 2000**.

Each procedure is described in detail and illustrated so that you can put it into action easily.

The final pages are given over to an **index** of the topics covered and a set of **appendices**, which give details of the toolbars and shortcut keys available in Project 2000.

The typographic conventions used in this book are as follows:

Type faces used for specific purposes:	
bold	indicates the option to take in a menu or dialog box.
italic	is used for notes and comments.
Ctrl	represents a key from the keyboard; when two keys appear side by side, they should be pressed simultaneously.
Symbols indicating the content of a paragraph:	
▒	an action to carry out (activating an option, clicking with the mouse...).
⇨	a general comment on the command in question.
↴	a technique which involves the mouse.
⬙	a keyboard technique.
▤	a technique wich uses options from the menus.

Microsoft Project 2000

Microsoft Project 2000

1.1 Principles of project management

A-Planning your project

▦ Before your project starts, it is vital to establish a plan, to clarify what the project involves and what its end objective is.

A plan does not say what will happen, but rather what you would like to happen. It informs all the actors in the project of what should happen, when and how. Each person involved can see how they fit into the project and what their exact role will be.

▦ A plan is only truly useful if it is updated regularly.

▦ The key points in a plan are:

Step 1: Make a list of tasks and milestones.
Step 2: Determine the relationship between each task.
Step 3: Estimate how long each task will take.
Step 4: Build your network diagram.
Step 5: Optimise your network diagram.

B-Listing tasks and milestones

▦ Each **activity** or **task** is the description of the work that needs to be done to obtain a specific result, for example, writing a user's manual for a machine.

▦ One or more **resources** are put to work on each task.

▦ The more detailed the task is, the easier it is to estimate the means required to carry it out.

Do not hesitate to replace a task by two or three more detailed tasks, although you should not take this to an extreme.

▦ A **milestone** is a task with a duration of zero, or a negligible duration in relation to the tasks around it. A milestone represents intermediate objectives that show more clearly how the project is progressing. This can mark the end of a particular series of activities, an external event etc.

▦ Each project should have a milestone to mark its start date and another to represent its completion.

C-Determining the relationships between tasks

▦ A **link** describes the order in which tasks should occur. A link does not usually have a duration.

In Microsoft Project 2000, four types of relationship can exist between tasks:

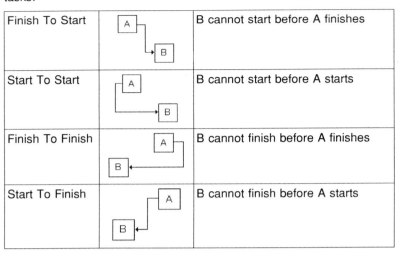

Finish To Start		B cannot start before A finishes
Start To Start		B cannot start before A starts
Finish To Finish		B cannot finish before A finishes
Start To Finish		B cannot finish before A starts

90% of links are of the "Finish To Start" type: the most rare type is the "Start To Finish" link. In Project, A is called the **predecessor** *and B the* **successor***.*

- Each task has its own identification number, which corresponds to its row number.
- For each task link, ask yourself, "what other tasks am I depending on to be able to start this task?".
- Except for the starting task and any external events, each task must have at least one predecessor.

D-Estimating task duration

- The **duration** is the amount of time separating the start and the end of a task. This depends on how much work needs to be carried out and what means are available to carry it out.
- To estimate a duration, use your own personal experience or get specialist advice; you can also apply the **Beta rule**. For each task, take these three durations: an optimistic (Do), a pessimistic (Dp) and an expected duration (De).
  You can then calculate (and use) an average duration (Da):
  $Da = (Do+Dp+4De)/6$.

E-Constructing a network

▓ You can show your task information as a Network Diagram (also called a PERT chart). Tasks are presented in boxes and arrows represent the links between them:

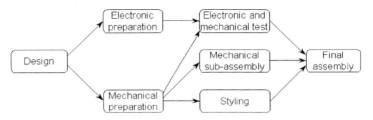

▓ Calculate the total duration of the project. This calculation is made in two phases, after you have omitted the milestones.

- First phase:

  Determine the earliest start date for each task. In most cases this is done according to the links established. When a task has several predecessors, take the one that finishes last.

- Second phase:

  You should work backwards from the finish date to calculate the latest start and finish dates. This helps you find the date at which each task should be finished so the project does not fall behind schedule.

  These calculations are easier to make if you add a successor column. When there are several successors, take into account the one that starts the earliest.

F-Levelling the network diagram

▓ Slack time refers to how long a task can slip behind without affecting the dates of another task or the project's end date. Two types exist: **total slack** and **free slack**.

- **Total slack** is the amount of time a task can slip without affecting the project finish date. It is the difference between a task's latest and earliest start dates.

- **Free slack** is the amount of time a task can be put back without making other tasks late. It is the difference between the earliest finish date of the task and the earliest start date of the earliest successor - (minus) 1.

▓ The sequence of tasks with a total slack of zero is called the **critical path**. Any change in the duration of one of these tasks has a direct effect on the project's finish date. These tasks are called **critical tasks**.

▓ Tasks can often have time gaps between them, known as lead **time** or **lag time**. An example of lag time: varnish is applied one week <u>after</u> the painting is finished. An example of lead time: manufacturing can start one week <u>before</u> the design stage is over.

G-Using calendars for time management

▧ Project 2000 schedules tasks by taking into account the work schedules of a number of resources. It works with a number of different calendars, associated with various elements (tasks, resources etc).

▧ Project 2000 uses **working time calendars** to know the number of hours in a working day, as well as which are working and nonworking days and hours and so on. There are two types of working time calendars:

- the **base calendar** (or project calendar) stores the working and non-working hours and days scheduled for several resources, generally those doing the same type of work or working on a group activity. The default base calendar used by Project 2000 is called **Standard**.

- the **resource calendar** contains the work schedule for a given resource or group of resources. The resource calendar is based on the Standard calendar but specifies its exceptions.

⇨ *Each calendar inherits the working and nonworking days of the calendar on which it is based. Any changes to the base calendar are carried over into the calendars derived from it. If you change the status of a day in the base calendar (by calling it a nonworking day for example), you change the working times of all the resources that rely on that calendar. This also affects the schedule for any task assigned to those resources on that particular day.*

1.2 The working environment

A-Starting/leaving Project 2000

▦ Click the **Start** button, point to the **Programs** option and choose **Microsoft Project**.

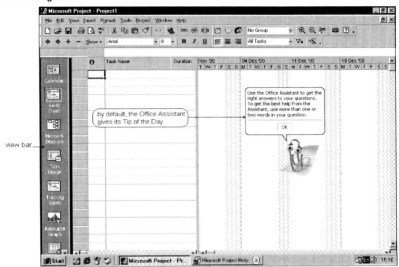

Apart from the Office Assistant, Project 2000 also offers you a help window, which can either be open or reduced to a button on the taskbar (a). This depends on your version of Windows.

▦ You can choose:

    (a)   to consult **What's New** in Project 2000,

(b)   to see a **Quick Preview** of the application's features,

(c)   to take a **Tutorial** to learn how to use Project,

(d)   to see an overview of project management using the **Project Map**,

(e)   to use the **Office Assistant** to get help,

(f)   to close the **Welcome** window.

▨ When you start Project, it generally shows you the project tasks in a view called the **Gantt Chart**. The left pane shows the task entry sheet, whose first column displays each task's name (scroll this pane horizontally to see the other columns it contains). The right pane shows the tasks in a chart representing the period around the current date of your computer.

▨ To leave Project 2000,

File	Click the ☒ button	⌨Alt ⌨F4
Quit	on the application window	

⇨ *To hide (or display) the **View Bar**, use the **View - View Bar** command.*

⇨ *To stop the help window appearing when you start Project, use **Tools - Options - General** tab and deactivate the **Display help at startup** option.*

⇨ *If you want the last file in which you were working to open automatically when Project 2000 starts, go into **Tools - Options - General** tab and activate **Open last file on startup**.*

B-Undoing your last action

▨ **Edit**	↶	⌨Ctrl **Z**
Undo		

⇨ *When you cancel an action, the **Undo** option becomes the **Redo** option and the* ↶ *tool button becomes* ↷ *. These both redo the action you just cancelled.*

1.3 Toolbars

A-Showing/hiding a toolbar

▨ **View - Toolbars**

▨ Click the name of the bar you wish to display (or hide).

⇨ *You can also right-click any toolbar currently displayed then choose the name of the toolbar to hide/show.*

B-Moving a toolbar

move handle

- Point to the move handle of the toolbar concerned and drag it to the required position:
    - to the left or right edge of the window to make it a vertical toolbar,
    - to the top or bottom of the window to make it a horizontal toolbar,
    - to the middle of the screen to make a floating toolbar (the tools appear in a window).
- ⇨ *You can also make a toolbar into a floating toolbar by double-clicking its move handle.*
- ⇨ *You can dock a floating toolbar by double-clicking its title bar.*

C-Creating a toolbar

- **View - Toolbars - Customize**
- Click the **New** button.

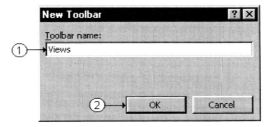

- ① Enter the name of the toolbar.
- ② Click to confirm.
- Add the required buttons to the toolbar.

D-Adding/removing toolbar buttons

▨ **View - Toolbars - Customize**

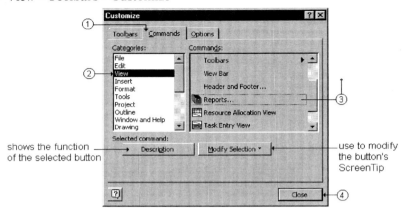

shows the function of the selected button

use to modify the button's ScreenTip

① Activate this tab.

② Select a category.

③ Select the button you want to add and drag it to the required toolbar.

④ Click to confirm.

⇨ *To remove a tool button from a toolbar, open the **Customize** dialog box and drag the button off the toolbar concerned.*

⇨ *Toolbar customisations are saved in the GLOBAL.MPT file and are then applied to all projects.*

2.1 Project files

A- Opening a project file

⬛ File
Open

Ctrl O

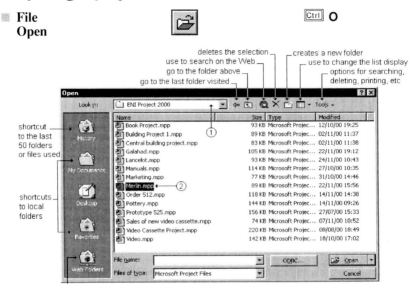

deletes the selection ─┐ ┌─ creates a new folder
use to search on the Web ─┐ │ ┌─ use to change the list display
go to the folder above ─┐ │ │ │ ┌─ options for searching,
go to the last folder visited ─┐ │ │ │ │ │ deleting, printing, etc

shortcut to the last 50 folders or files used

shortcuts to local folders

└ shortcut to Web folders on a server

① Go to the drive and folder where the file is located.

② Double-click the name of the file you want to open.

⇨ *The drop-down list on the* ***Open*** *button can be used to open a file in read-only mode or open a copy of the file.*

⇨ *The list of the last four files used can be found in the* ***File*** *menu. The number of documents given depends on the choice made in* ***Tools - Options - General*** *tab,* ***Recently used file list*** *option.*

B- Closing a project file

⬛ File
Close

Click the button on the document window

Ctrl F4

⬛ If necessary, save any changes made.

C- Creating a new project file

⬛ File
New

Ctrl N

fill in the project information

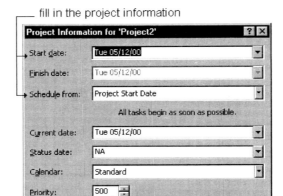

⮕ *If you do not wish to fill in the **Project Information** when you create a new project, you can stop this dialog box appearing: use **Tools - Options - General** tab and deactivate **Prompt for project info for new projects**.*

D-Activating a file which is open in the background

▓ Open the **Window** menu:

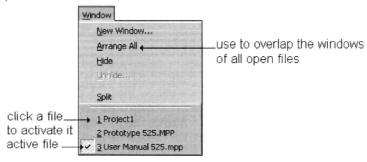

use to overlap the windows of all open files

click a file to activate it

active file

⮕ *The **Window - Hide** command hides the active window without closing it. To display it again, use **Window - Unhide**.*

⮕ *On the keyboard, use* Ctrl F6 *to activate the next document and* Ctrl ⇧ Shift F6 *to activate the previous one.*

⮕ *You can also activate an open file by clicking the corresponding button on the taskbar. This is possible only with some versions of Windows.*

E-Saving a project

▓ **File**
Save

Ctrl **S**

If the file is being saved for the first time, fill in this dialog box:

click to create a new folder if required

① Select the drive then the folder in which you want to save the file.

② Give your project's name (up to 255 characters, including spaces).

③ Click to save the project.

When the Planning Wizard opens, choose to **Save without a baseline** if your project is not yet in its realisation phase then enter.

⇨ *Project automatically gives project files the .mpp extension.*

⇨ *The **File - Save As** command can be used to save the project under another name.*

⇨ *The **Planning Wizard** dialog box appears during saving only if the **Advice from Planning Wizard** option is active in **Tools - Options - General** tab.*

F-Restricting access to a project

File - Save As

Click the **Tools** button then choose **General Options**.

the characters you enter appear as asterisks

① Depending on what restriction you are imposing, use the following options:

(a)　　enter the password required to open the project.

(b)　　enter the password required to make changes to the project (if the user cannot supply this password, the project opens in read-only mode).

② Tick this option if Project 2000 should recommend to users opening the file that they open it in read-only mode.

③ Confirm.

⇨ *Project differentiates between upper and lower case in passwords.*

G-Setting file saving preferences

▒ **Tools - Options - Save** tab

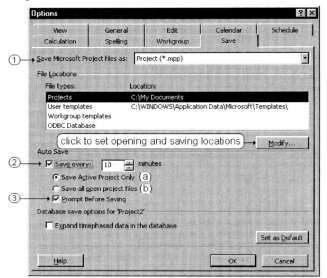

① Choose the default file type to use when saving project files.

② Tick this option to activate automatic saving then specify if it should save only the active project (a) or all open projects (b).

③ Should Project ask you to confirm before saving automatically?

H-Saving information in HTML format

▒ **File - Save As Web Page**

▒ If necessary, modify the **File name** then make sure **Save as type** is set to **Web Page (*.html;*.htm)**.

▒ In the **Save in** box, modify the folder in which to save the file (if necessary).

▒ Click the **Save** button.

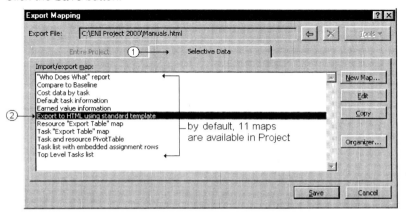

① Activate this tab.

② Choose the map Project 2000 should use to select the information that will then appear in the HTML file using a preset template.

▒ Click **OK**.

I- Exporting Project data to Excel using a predefined map

▒ Open the project containing the data you want to export.

▒ **File - Save As**

▒ Open the **Save as type** drop-down list and choose one of the formats:

Microsoft Excel Worksheet to export to a worksheet.

Microsoft Excel PivotTable to export to a pivot table.

▒ Give the name of the exported file in the **File name** box.

▒ If necessary, use the **Save in** box to specify the name of the folder where you want to save the exported file.

▒ Click the **Save** button.

▒ In the **Export Mapping** dialog box, choose one of the 11 preset import/export maps and click **Save**.

J- Publishing a project in a new Web folder

▒ Ensure the project looks as you want it to appear on the Web server.

▒ **File - Save As**

▒ Click the [Web Folders] shortcut on the **Places Bar**.

▒ To create a new Web folder, click the **Create New Folder** tool button to start the appropriate wizard.

- In the **Add Web Folder** dialog box, **Type the location to add** in the corresponding text box or click the **Browse** button to look for a location with your browser.
- Click the **Next** button.
- If you wish, **Enter the name for this Web Folder** in the corresponding text box and click the **Finish** button.

  By default, Project 2000 suggests using the URL address as the folder name. The Web folder and its supporting files are then created.
- In the **Save As** dialog box, modify the **File name** that will be published on the server (if required) and click **Save**.

2.2 Templates and workspaces

A-Creating a project template

You can use a template when you create several projects with a similar structure of tasks or elements (calendars, reports etc) or that use a similar group of resources.

- In a new project, create these common elements (tasks, resources, calendars and so on).
- **File - Save As**

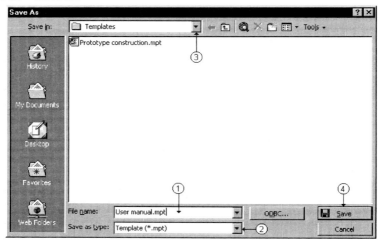

① Enter the file name.

② Open the list and choose the **Template (*.mpt)** option.

③ If necessary, select another place to save the file, but it is a good idea to keep all templates in the **Templates** folder.

④ Click to confirm.

⇨ *To modify a project template, open it as any other project file, make the required changes then save it with the* 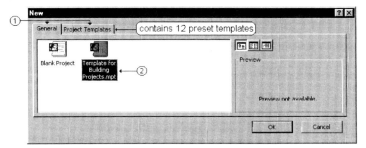 *tool button.*

⇨ *By default, Project 2000 saves templates in the **Templates** folder (whose full path is C:\Windows\Application Data\Microsoft\Templates).*

B-Using a project template

▓ **File - New**

① Activate the tab in which the template is located.

② Double-click the template you want to use.

▓ Work in your project then save it with the tool button.

⇨ *If you need to use a template which is not saved in the **Templates** folder, you will need to use **File - Open** to open the template then **File - Save As** to create your new file.*

C-Customising future new projects

▓ Using the **Tools - Organizer** dialog box, copy all the elements that will be common to all new projects into the **GLOBAL.MPT** file (cf. "Copying elements from one project to another").

▓ Once you have made your copy, click the **Close** button.

D-Creating a workspace

A workspace is a group of files that you open simultaneously in a predefined working environment.

▓ Open the projects concerned and arrange the windows and views as you want them to look in the workspace.

▓ **File - Save Workspace**

▓ Give a **File name** and indicate where to save the workspace file.

▓ Click the **Save** button.

⇨ *You can open a workspace as you would any other file; this type of file carries an .mpw extension.*

3.1 Project characteristics

A-Adding notes to a project

▨ **File - Properties**

▨ If necessary, activate the **Summary** tab and fill in the various characteristics of the project.

B-Setting project dates

▨ **Project - Project Information**

▨ Open the **Schedule from** list and choose either **Project Start Date** or
Project Finish Date.

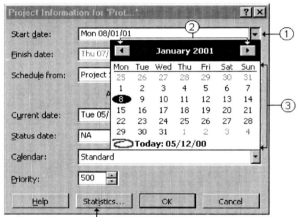

Lclick to show the project statistics

▨ To indicate the start date or finish date, click in the appropriate text box
then:

① Open the calendar.

② Display the month of your choice.

③ Click the required date.

▨ Click **OK**.

⇨ *You can also enter a date directly in the required text box.*

⇨ *When you specify a start date, the end date is calculated from the links
between tasks, constraints and so on.*

⇨ *When you schedule a finish date, all tasks become critical as they are
scheduled to begin as late as possible!*

C-Customising the project's base calendar

By default the working days defined by Project 2000 in the Standard calendar are Monday to Friday. Working hours are 8.00 till 12.00 and 13.00 till 17.00, giving a 40-hour working week. No holidays or public holidays are scheduled. Each calendar begins January 1, 1984 and ends 31 December, 2049.

Defining non-working days

▓ **Tools - Change Working Time**

▓ Check that your changes will be **For: Standard (Project Calendar)**.

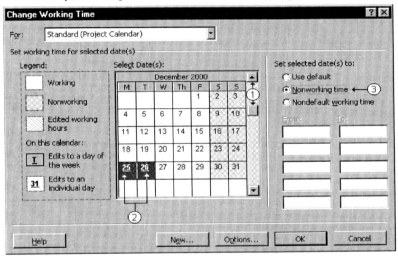

① Show the required month and year.

② Select with ⬆Shift-clicks or Ctrl-clicks the working days that should become non-working days.

③ Activate this option.

⇨ *It is a good idea to set up calendars for a longer period than the initially planned project period, as projects are frequently late!*

Defining working hours

click here to select every Monday in the year

Change Working Time		? X

For: Standard (Project Calendar) ▼

Set working time for selected date(s)

Legend:

☐ Working
☐ Nonworking
☐ Edited working hours

On this calendar:

⊥ Edits to a day of the week
31 Edits to an individual day

Select Date(s):

October 2000

	M	T	W	Th	F	S	S
							1
2	3	4	5	6	7	8
9	10	11	12	13	14	15
16	17	18	19	20	21	22
23	24	25	26	27	28	29
30	31					

Set selected date(s) to:

○ Use default
○ Nonworking time
● Nondefault working time

From: To:
08:30   12:00
13:00   17:00

Help   New...   Options...   OK   Cancel

① Select the days which will have different working hours.

② Give the new work shifts then remove the current selection by clicking elsewhere in the calendar (up to five work shifts can be entered, which is especially useful for projects involving night or shift work).

⇨ *When you create half-working days, be careful to delete the other hours correctly (do not use spaces). The first row must not be empty; if no work is programmed in the morning, enter the afternoon hours in the first row and empty all the others.*

⇨ *Any changes made in this dialog box affect the start and end dates of each task and often affect the project finish date.*

Printing the calendar

▦ **View - Reports**

▦ Double-click **Overview** then **Working Days**.

▦ In the print preview, click the **Print** button and confirm with **OK**.

D-Modifying the general calendar options

▦ **Tools - Options - Calendar** tab

▦ Update the calendar options of your choice.

⇨ *It is better to modify the general calendar options before creating the list of tasks (especially in relation to their duration).*

E-Making a project calendar into the global calendar

▓ **Tools - Organizer - Calendars** tab

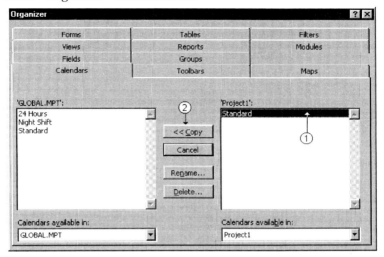

① Select the calendar you wish to copy.

② Copy the selected calendar into the GLOBAL.MPT base.

⇨ *If the copied calendar's name already exists in the base, Project will show you this message:*

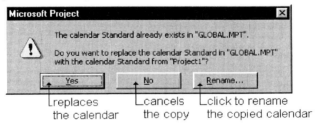

└replaces   └cancels   └click to rename
the calendar   the copy   the copied calendar

▓▓3.2 Project elements

A-Copying elements from one project to another

▓ Open the project containing the element you wish to copy and the destination project for that copy.

If the list of resources is shared over several projects, you can open it in one of several ways:

(a)   in read-only mode so other users can work on projects connected with the list.

(b)   in read-write mode, so you can modify the resource information. While the file is open, other projects cannot add information to the list of resources.

(c)   This option opens simultaneously the resource list file and all the other projects that share that file within the consolidated project.

Tools - Organizer

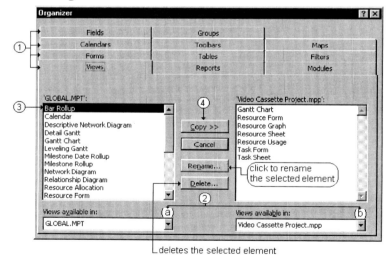

① Activate the appropriate tab for the element you wish to copy.

② Show (a) the source project and (b) the destination project.

③ Click the element you are copying.

④ Click this button.

B-Customising project elements

*First, ask yourself: Do I want to **create** a completely new element or a new one based on an existing element, or do I simply want to **modify** an existing element?*

To create or copy elements, use the appropriate technique for the type of element:

Type of element	Technique
Task table or resource table	- Show the tasks/resources - **View - Table - More Tables** - If creating, click the **Create** button - If copying, select the table concerned and click **Copy**
Task filter or resource filter	- Show the tasks/resources - **Project - Filtered for - More Filters** - If creating, click the **Create** button - If copying, select the filter concerned and click **Copy**
Report	- **View - Reports - Custom** - If creating, click the **Create** button - If copying, select the report concerned and click **Copy**
View	- **View - More Views** - If creating, click the **Create** button - If copying, select the view concerned and click **Copy**

If you are modifying, the technique depends on whether you modify an element's presentation or contents.

Contents can be modified using the menus mentioned above; select each element concerned then click the **Edit** button.

3.3 Linked and consolidated projects

A-Creating a subproject task

*To work on a large project with several distinct phases, you can create a separate project for each phase and then work on these **subprojects** as tasks in another project called the **master project**.*

In the main project, create the list of tasks without worrying about the subproject tasks.

In the list, click the task that will follow the task you are creating.

Insert - Project

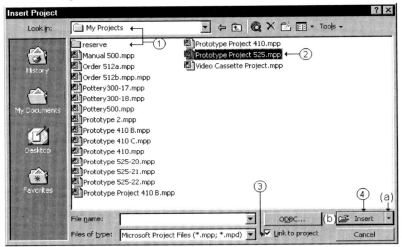

① Activate the folder where the subproject file is stored.

② Select the name of the subproject.

③ If you do not want changes made to the subproject from the main file to be carried over into the subproject file and vice-versa, deactivate this option.

④ If you do not want to be able to modify the subproject from the main file, open the drop-down list (a) then click the **Insert Read-Only** option. To insert the project in a standard way, just click **Insert** (b).

If necessary, update the links between tasks.

⇨ *The duration of a subproject task equals the total duration of that subproject file. The task appears as a summary task in the main project. The subproject task takes the name of the subproject file.*

⇨ *In the ⓘ column, the 🖼 icon indicates tasks that contain subprojects and the 🖼 icon tasks that have inserted subprojects in read-only mode. Tasks that contain an inserted project unrelated to the original project are considered as ordinary tasks, not as subproject tasks.*

B-Consolidating several individual projects

You can consolidate a number of separate projects to review them in terms of time and resources and produce reports on them more easily.

Open the projects you wish to consolidate.

Window - New Window

22

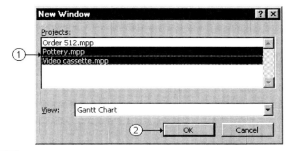

① Use ⌜Ctrl⌝-clicks to choose each project to include in the consolidation.

② Confirm.

⇨ *Unless you specify otherwise, project summary tasks are linked to their source files and can be modified from the consolidated project.*

⇨ *You can set up links between the tasks of the different projects.*

C-Exploring a consolidated project

▓ In the Gantt sheet:

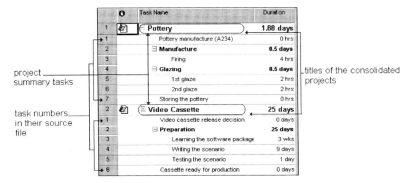

▓ In the Gantt chart, project summary bars look like other task summary bars except they are coloured grey instead of black.

D-Saving a consolidated project

▓ Save the consolidated file as you would any other file.

▓ Accept or refuse to save each source file.

▓ If Project prompts you, specify if you want to save the projects with or without a baseline.

E-Modifying the links between a project and a source file

░ Double-click the project summary task.

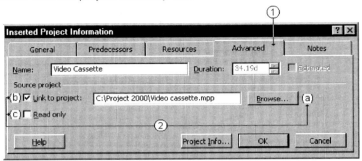

① Activate this tab.

② Change one or other of the following options:

a)   if the source file has changed or been moved, update its name (or file path).

b)   deactivate this option if the project summary task should no longer be linked to the source file.

c)   activate this option to prevent the source file being modified from the main (or consolidated) file.

F-Showing the names of subproject files in the Gantt chart

░ Show the Gantt chart concerned.

░ **Format - Bar Styles**

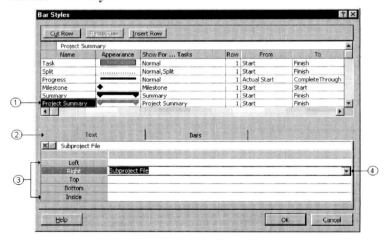

① Select the project summary bars.

② Activate this tab.

③ Choose where the file names should appear in relation to the bar.

④ Open the list and select this option.

⇨ *The subproject file names appear preceded by their file paths.*

G-Showing subproject statistics

▧ Double-click the subproject task concerned.

▧ Click the **Project Info** button.

*If the **Project Info** button is unavailable, close the **Inserted Project Information** window, expand the subproject details by clicking the corresponding plus (+) sign then collapse the details with the minus (-) sign and double-click the subproject again.*

▧ Click the **Statistics** button.

▧ To leave the statistics, use **Close - Cancel**.

3.4 Sharing resources

A-Sharing resources between projects

▧ Open the file containing the resources you want to share (the resource pool) and the file that wants to use those resources (the sharer file).

▧ Activate the sharer file.

▧ **Tools - Resources**

▧ Choose the **Share Resources** option.

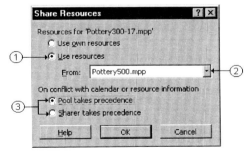

① Activate this option.

② Select the source file.

③ Indicate which file takes precedence in the case of a conflict. If the first option is active, the resource pool takes priority, if the second is active, the active file (the sharer) takes precedence.

⇨ *You can access shared resources from all projects. The **Resource Usage** view lists all the tasks to which the resources have been assigned.*

⇨ *When you save projects that share resources, Project asks how it should save your changes:*

B-Managing shared resources

▨ Open a resource pool as you would any other project.

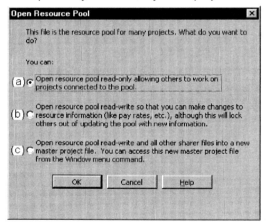

▨ Choose:

    (a)   to open the list in read-only mode.

    (b)   to open the list in read/write mode.

    (c)   to open the list and all other sharer files.

To open a sharer file, proceed as for any other project file.

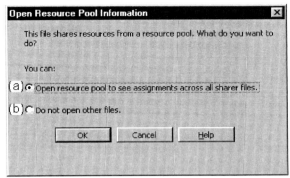

Choose:

(a)   to open the resource pool and the sharer files.

(b)   to open only the sharer file.

To modify a shared resource, open the resource pool and the sharer files then modify the resource from any of these projects.

C-Grouping tasks or resources

In Project 2000, you can group tasks or resources according to your own criteria without changing the basic structure of your project.

To group tasks, display them in the task sheet (**View - More Views - Task Sheet - Apply**) or in the Gantt chart (**View - Gantt Chart**).

Project - Group by

Click one of the grouping criteria shown in the menu or click the **More Groups** option to see the full list of groups.

In the **More Groups** window, activate either **Task** or **Resource** as appropriate then click the group that meets your view requirements. Click the **Apply** button.

⇨ *To cancel your grouping and return to the normal view of tasks or resources, use* ***Project - Group by - No Group.***

4.1 The Gantt Chart

A-Showing the Gantt Chart

▨ **View - Gantt Chart** or ▣

⇨ *To see only the task entry sheet element of the view, use* ***View - More Views*** *and double-click* ***Task Sheet.***

B-Moving around in the Gantt Chart

▨ To move within the task sheet, use the following keys:

Ctrl Home / Ctrl End	First/last column of the first/last task.
Home / End	First/last column in the current row.
Ctrl Pg Up / Ctrl Pg Dn	Next screen page to the left/right.
Pg Dn / Pg Up	Next screen page down/up.

▨ In the chart pane, drag the horizontal scroll bar to find the time period you require.

▨ To see a specific task bar, select the task in the left pane and click the

Go To Selected Task ▣ tool button.

▨ **Edit - Go To** or Ctrl **G**

▨ Enter the task's **ID** number or its **Date** and confirm with Enter .

⇨ *With this technique you move to the given place in both the task sheet and the chart.*

C-Zooming the Gantt Chart

▨ **View - Zoom**

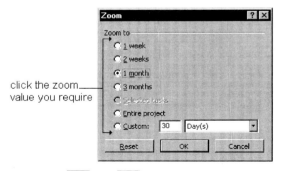

click the zoom
value you require

⇨ *You can also use the* ⊕ *and* ⊖ *tool buttons.*

D-Printing the Gantt Chart

▧ Start by opening a print preview: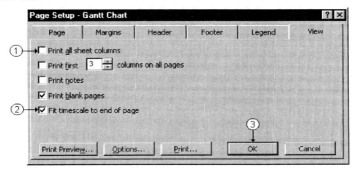

▧ To print all the columns from the task sheet: click the **Page Setup** button, **View** tab.

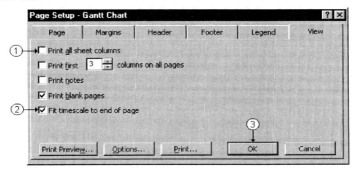

① Tick this option.

② Check that this option is active.

③ Confirm.

▧ Start printing by clicking **Print** then **OK**.

E-Modifying the Gantt Chart timescale

▧ **Format - Timescale**

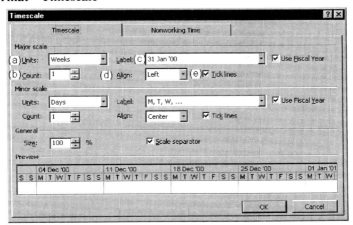

▧ On the **Timescale** page, modify the setup of the timescale as required, using these options:

(a)   defines the time unit to use (**Years, Half Years, Quarters, Months, Thirds of Months, Weeks, Days, Hours, Minutes**). The minor scale units should be smaller than or equal to the major scale units.

(b)   defines how frequently the chosen unit should be displayed.

(c)   defines the format of the unit label.

(d)   defines whether the unit is centred, right or left aligned.

(e)   defines whether or not separation lines appear between the unit labels.

▓ Click the **Nonworking Time** tab and set the following options:

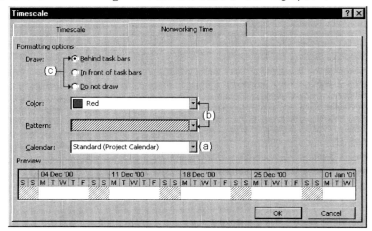

(a)   specify which calendar to use to locate the nonworking periods.

(b)   choose the colour and pattern in which the nonworking periods should appear.

(c)   choose not to draw these periods or to put them behind or in front of the task bars.

⇨ *Changing the **Units** and **Count** settings automatically alters the zoom settings and vice-versa.*

F-Changing the way the current date appears in the Gantt

▓ **Format - Gridlines**

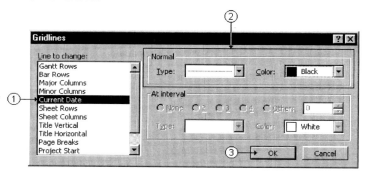

① Choose this option.

② Specify the presentation of the date line.

③ Confirm.

⇨ *You can use the **Normal** and **At interval** frames in this dialog box to change the format of other lines, if you wish.*

G-Formatting dates and the Gantt bars

▓ **Format - Layout**

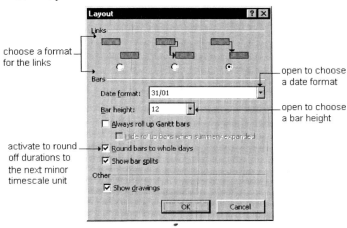

choose a format for the links

open to choose a date format

open to choose a bar height

activate to round off durations to the next minor timescale unit

VIEWS

H-Modifying text format

▓ **Format - Text Styles**

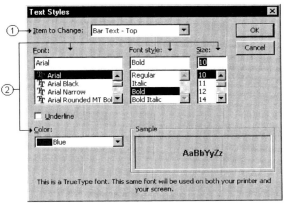

① Choose the element whose text style is to be modified.

② Modify the appearance of the text in question.

I- Changing the look of the Gantt bars

Open the **Format** menu. To work on a previously selected task bar, choose **Bar**. To change a category of task bar, choose **Bar Styles**.

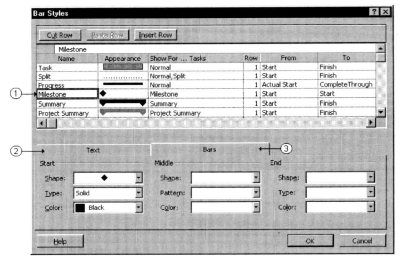

① Select the category of bar you want to modify. To specify your own task category, click the first empty cell in the **Name** column and give the new task group a name (this is important as this name appears on the legend when you print the chart). Open the list in **Show For ... Tasks** in the current row and select the type of task represented by your new category (if the category represents several tasks, list them with a comma separating each one).

② Use the options under this tab to give the location and content of the text.

③ Use the options under this tab to specify the appearance of the bars.

⇨ *Yes/No fields are the only custom fields that you can represent differently on the Gantt Chart. Project applies a different presentation when the task's **Indicator** field contains **Yes**. If you want negations to appear, use the "Not" keyword.*

4.2 Task organisation

A-Viewing and understanding the Network Diagram

▨ **View - Network Diagram** or

If you installed Project 2000 as an update of a previous version, the ***PERT Chart*** *option may appear instead of the* ***Network Diagram*** *option in the* ***View Bar*** *and the* ***View*** *menu. The Network Diagram used to be called the PERT Chart.*

Even if your version of Project 2000 is not an update but you are using files created on a previous version, you may still see the ***PERT Chart*** *icon or option appear in the* ***View Bar*** *and* ***View*** *menu.*

▨ The Network Diagram shows each task in a box, containing the task name, its duration, its start and finish dates, and the resources that have been assigned to it.

▨ The boxes for tasks on the critical path are outlined in red.

▨ The Network Diagram also shows the links (or dependency) between the tasks. This allows you to check that no task has been left out. Except for the first and last task, every task must have at least one predecessor and one successor.

▨ Use these keys to move within the diagram:

Ctrl Home / Ctrl End   shows the first/last tasks.

↓ / ↑ / → / ←   selects the next box.

▨ To define a finish to start type link, click the predecessor task box. When the pointer becomes a white cross, drag towards the successor task.

⇨ *You can use the* ***View - Zoom*** *command to zoom the diagram.*

⇨ *Dotted lines represent page breaks that will appear during printing.*

B-Moving Network Diagram boxes

▨ **Format - Layout**

▨ Under **Layout Mode**, activate the **Allow manual box positioning** option and click **OK**.

▨ Point at the border of the box that you want to move.

▨ When the pointer appears as a black four-headed arrow, drag the box to the required position.

C-Customising the Network Diagram

▦ To align the task boxes horizontally in chronological order, use **Format - Layout now**.

▦ To change the look of the linking arrows, use **Format - Layout**.

choose one
of these options

▦ To change the look of the boxes, use **Format - Box Styles**.

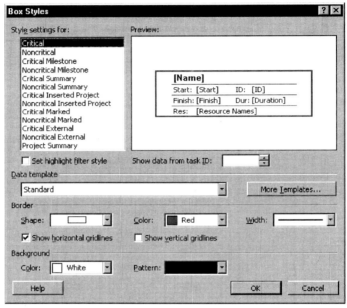

▦ Set the options for the presentation you require.

4.3 Calendar view

A-Displaying the calendar

▓ View - Calendar or ▓

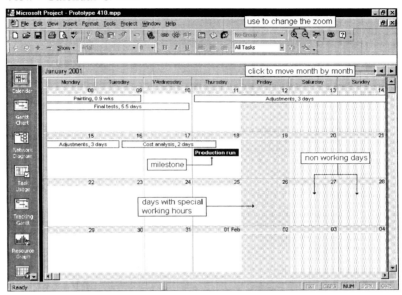

▓ For each task, a task bar covers the days or weeks over which that task is scheduled.

▓ To see more details of the tasks scheduled on a particular date, double-click the number of that day.

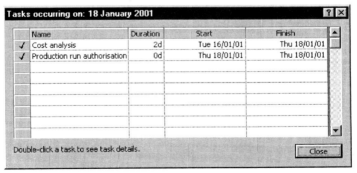

⇨ *You can also modify the zoom on the calendar with* **View - Zoom**. *These zoom values are based on the notion of time.*

B-Changing the calendar's timescale

Format - Timescale

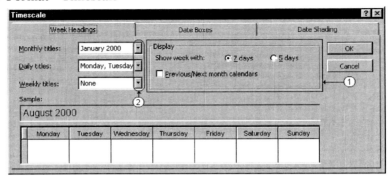

① Choose the number of days to show per week.

② Choose the format for the weekly row titles in Calendar view.

C-Printing the calendar

▨ Start the print preview with [icon].

▨ To reduce the number of pages printed, click the **Page Setup** button and activate the **View** tab.

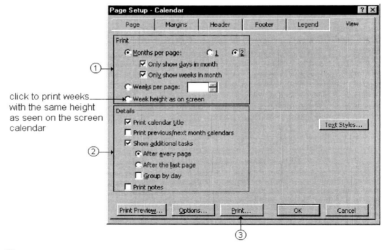

① Choose what you want to print on each page.

② Specify what other elements should be printed.

③ Start printing then click **OK** to confirm.

⇨ *When printing two months per page, Project 2000 may print a month lying outside the project period.*

4.4 Customised views

A-Modifying the date display format

- Tools - Options
- If necessary, activate the **View** tab.
- Specify your preferred **Date format**.
- Click **OK**.

B-Creating a single view

- View - More Views - New - Single view - OK

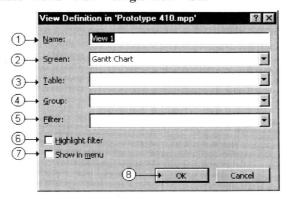

① Give your new view a name.

② Indicate the type of screen.

③ If Project allows you to, indicate which table to associate.

④ Specify the group concerned by the view.

⑤ Choose which filter you want to apply.

⑥ Tick this option to highlight the tasks or resources that meet the filter criteria.

⑦ Tick this option to make this view's name appear in the **View** menu and in the **View Bar**.

⑧ Click to confirm.

- Choose to **Apply** your changes or **Close**.

C-Creating a combination view

- View - More Views - New - Combination view - OK

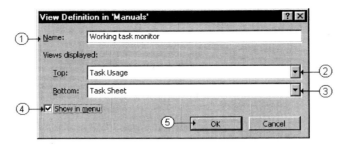

① Give the view a name.

② Choose what should appear in the top half of the screen.

③ Choose a view for the bottom half of the screen.

④ Tick if the view should appear in the **View** menu.

⑤ Confirm.

▓ Choose to **Apply** or **Close**.

D-Creating a new group

▓ Display the tasks (**Task Sheet** or **Gantt Chart**) or resources (**Resource Sheet** or **Resource Usage**).

▓ **Project - Group by - More Groups**

▓ Activate **Task** or **Resource** as appropriate.

▓ Click the **New** button.

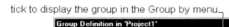

tick to display the group in the Group by menu

① Enter the group name.

② Use lists (a) and (b) to specify the grouping criteria.

③ Confirm.

5.1 Printing a project

A-Using the print preview

File - Print Preview or

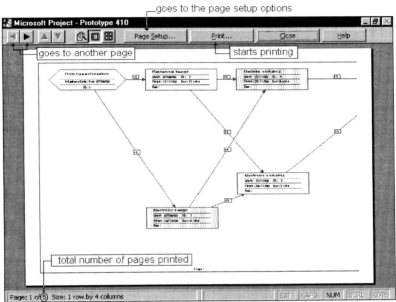

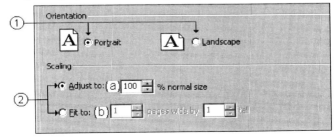

goes to the page setup options

goes to another page

starts printing

total number of pages printed

To zoom in on part of a page, place the pointer over the area and click.

To zoom out again, click the page once more.

B-Customising page setup

File - Page Setup or click the **Page Setup** button in the print preview.

To change the page orientation or printing scale, activate the **Page** tab.

① Choose the required page orientation.

② If necessary, modify the printing scale, either by entering a percentage by which to reduce or increase the document when printed (a) or by adjusting the size so all the data is printed in a specific number of pages (b).

▓ To change the margins, activate the **Margins** tab of the **Page Setup** dialog box and give the sizes of the **Top**, **Bottom**, **Left** or **Right** margins.

▓ To change the page borders, activate the **Margins** tab of the **Page Setup** dialog box.

specify the required___
type of border

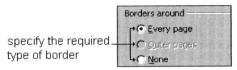

▓ To modify the page header/footer, activate the **Header** or **Footer** tab of the **Page Setup** dialog box.

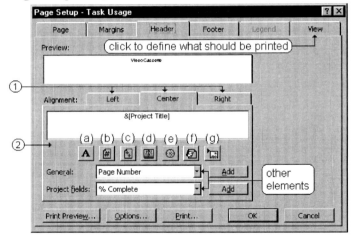

① Activate the required alignment for the header/footer item.

② Enter the header or footer text or a special item by clicking one of these buttons:

(a) a choice of fonts,   (e) the time,

(b) the page number,   (f) the name of the project file,

(c) the total number of pages, (g) a picture.

(d) the date,

▓ To modify the legend, activate the **Legend** tab of the **Page Setup** dialog box. Work on the general legend setup as you would for a header or footer. Define where you want your legend to appear using the **Legend on** options.

5.2 Reports

A-Customising reports

- View - Reports
- Double-click the **Custom** button.
- Click **New, Edit** or **Copy.**

B-Creating a report

- View - Reports - Custom - New

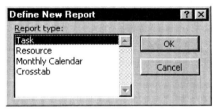

Creating a simple report

- In the **Define New Report** dialog box, select **Task** or **Resource** according to the data used and click **OK.**

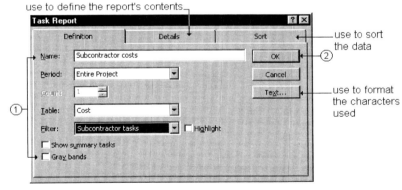

① Specify the report's name and contents.

② Confirm creating the report.

- Choose to **Print** the report or see a **Preview.**

Creating a crosstab report

▓ In the **Define New Report** dialog box, double-click **Crosstab**.

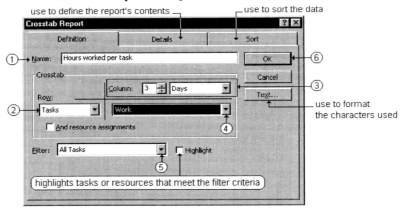

① Enter the report's name.

② Give the origin of the data to be presented in rows.

③ Indicate the time period for the analysis.

④ Choose the field you want to analyse.

⑤ If required, apply a filter.

⑥ Confirm creating the crosstab report.

▓ Choose to **Print** or **Preview** the report.

6.1 Managing tables

A-Creating a table

If you are creating a task table, display the tasks.
If you are creating a resource table, display the resources.

View - Table - More Tables

Choose to **Copy** a table or create a **New** one.

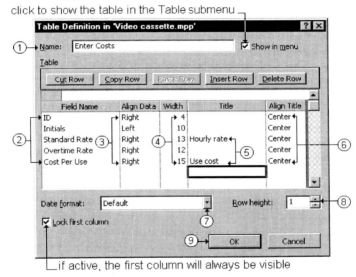

click to show the table in the Table submenu

if active, the first column will always be visible

① Give the new table a name.

② For each column in the table, select a field name.

③ Choose how to set out the data in each column.

④ Specify each column's default width.

⑤ If required, enter the intended label for each column (if this cell is empty, Project will use the field name as the label). Be careful if you enter label names; when Project makes a sort, it will only offer field names and not labels.

⑥ If necessary, choose the type of alignment for the column header.

⑦ If you want date fields to have a particular format, choose one here.

⑧ If necessary, modify the row height.

⑨ Click to confirm.

Click **Apply** or **Close**.

⇨ *A description of some task fields:*

Field type	Field Name	Comments
Numerical	*Number1 to Number20*	*for storing numbers*
Cost	*Cost1 to Cost10*	*for storing numbers in monetary format. This data is not taken into account in the total cost.*
Yes/No	*Flag1 to Flag20*	*for entering only "Yes" or "No" values.*
Text	*Text1 to Text30*	*You can enter up to 255 characters.*
Date	*Date1 to Date10*	*For storing dates.*
Code	*Outline Code1 to Outline Code10*	*For storing outline code information.*

⇨ *Here are some resource fields that can be customised:*

Text type   *Text1 to Text30*
Number type   *Number1 to Number20*
Cost type   *Cost1 to Cost10*
Yes/No type   *Flag1 to Flag20.*

B-Modifying the contents of a table

▓ To change the contents of a column, double-click the header of the column in question.

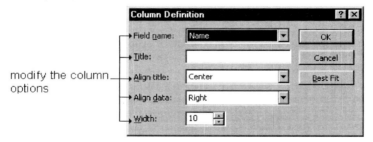

modify the column options

▓ To insert a column, click the header of the column that should follow the new one and use **Insert - Column** or ⎿Ins⏋. Give the characteristics of the new column and enter.

▓ To delete a column, click its header and use **Edit - Hide Column** or ⎿Del⏋.

▓ To move a column, use **View - Table - More Tables**, select the name of the table concerned and click the **Edit** button. Click a cell in the column you want to move then click the **Cut Row** button. Click the destination row for the data then the **Paste Row** button. Click **OK** and then **Apply**, or **Close**.

C-Resizing columns and pane

- To change a column's width, point to the vertical line to the right of its column header. When the pointer becomes a double-headed arrow, drag to change the width or double-click to make the column fit its longest entry.
- To change how panes are split, point to the appropriate split bar and drag in the correct direction.

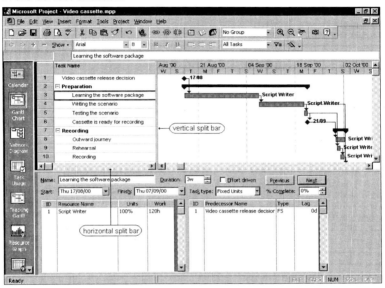

⇨ *Double-click a vertical split bar to align it to the nearest column border.*

⇨ *Double-clicking a horizontal split bar removes the window split.*

D-Modifying the gridlines on a table

- **Format - Gridlines**

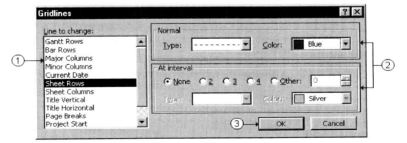

① Choose the type of line you want to modify.

② Change its formatting options.

③ Confirm your changes.

E-Modifying text format

▨ If you are working on the text in a particular row in the table, select the row and use **Format - Font**.

▨ If you are working on the text used for a specific type of data, use **Format - Text Styles**.

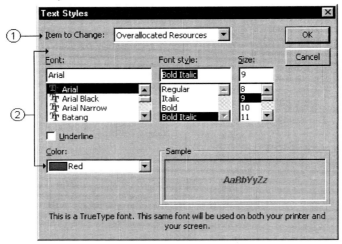

① Choose the element you want to modify.

② Set the required formatting options.

⇨ *When you change the look of a table, this applies to the tables of the current category (tasks or resources) and not just the current table.*

6.2 Managing cells

A-Modifying the contents of a cell

▨ Select the cell whose contents you want to modify.

▨ Click in the entry bar at the place where you want to make your changes or press F2.

▨ Make the required changes then enter.

⇨ *To delete preceding characters while you are typing, press the ⟵ key.*

B-Deleting the contents of a cell

- Click the cell whose contents you want to delete.
- Press the ⬅ key on the alphanumerical keyboard, or use Ctrl Del.
- To move to another cell, press Enter or press an arrow key.

⇨ *Be careful not to press the Del key alone; this will delete the contents of the current row.*

C-Copying the contents of a cell to adjacent cells

- Select the cell from which you want to copy and the destination cells for the copied material.

  The cell you are copying must be directly above, below or to the left or right of the destination cells.

  The destination cells do not have to be contiguous (but you must then select them with Ctrl -clicks).

- **Edit - Fill**
- Choose the direction for the copy.

⇨ *You can use the Ctrl B shortcut key to copy downwards.*

6.3 Using filters

A-Highlighting filtered tasks or resources

You can use filters to view a subset of tasks or resources, or to change the presentation of a subset of rows, while continuing to view the other rows.

- **Project - Filtered for - More Filters**
- Select the name of the filter that you want to apply.
- Apply the highlighting filter by clicking the **Highlight** button.

⇨ *By default, highlighting on filtered rows is applied in blue. You can change this colour with **Format - Text Styles - Item to Change: Highlighted Tasks** (or **Resources**).*

B-Customising a filter

- **Project - Filtered for - More Filters**

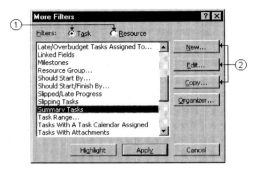

① Indicate which type of filter interests you.

② Choose which operation you wish to perform.

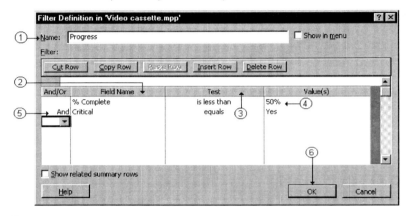

① Give a name to the filter.

② To set a condition, open the list and choose the field to which you want to apply your criterion.

③ Choose the operator that you want to use.

④ Enter or select the comparison value(s). To use the **is within** and **is not within** tests, you must specify a range of values. Enter the lower value, a semi-colon then the higher value. You can also use the * and ? wildcards. To compare your field with another field, open the list: the field names appear in square brackets.

⑤ To set several filter criteria, indicate whether all the test criteria must be satisfied (**And**) or only one of them (**Or**).

⑥ Enter.

▓ Choose to **Apply** the filter or to **Close**.

⇨ *To create an interactive filter (a filter that allows users to specify their own criteria), go to the **Value(s)** cell in the condition you want to make interactive then enter between quotation marks the message that will guide the users. Immediately after the closing quotation marks, enter a question mark.*

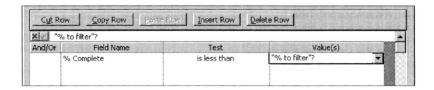

C-Using Autofilters

To activate/deactivate the Autofilters, click .

down arrows appear to the right of each column header

To filter by a column value, click the arrow on the column concerned.

cancels the column's filter

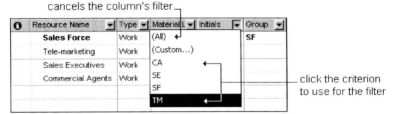

click the criterion
to use for the filter

When a filter is in use, the arrow and the column header appear in blue.

To combine criteria on different fields with an "And", set your conditions in each column concerned.

To combine two criteria on the same field, click the arrow button for the column concerned, and choose **(Custom...)**.

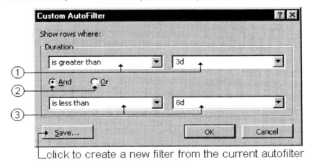

click to create a new filter from the current autofilter

① Set your first condition.

② Specify how the criteria should be combined.

③ Set your second condition.

7.1 Defining tasks

A-Entering the task names for a project

▒ In the **Entry Table** of the **Gantt Chart**, activate the first cell in the **Task Name** column.

▒ Enter the **Task Name**.

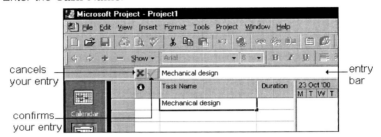

▒ Confirm your entry with ⌨Enter or ⌨↓.

The duration of the confirmed task goes to 1 day and a bar appears in the right pane of the Gantt Chart.

▒ Using the same technique, enter the various tasks of your project.

⇨ *If the entry bar does not appear, use* **Tools - Options - View** *tab and activate the* **Entry bar** *check box.*

⇨ *If the next cell down is not activated when you press the* ⌨Enter *key, use* **Tools - Options - Edit** *tab and activate the* **Move selection after enter** *option.*

B-Defining and working with milestones

▒ A milestone is a special task, with a duration of zero. To create a milestone, simply enter zero as the duration of a task.

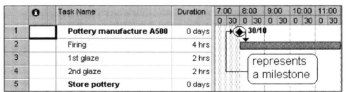

▒ To transform a task into a milestone, double-click the task concerned. Under the **Advanced** tab, tick the **Mark task as milestone** option and enter.

A diamond shape appears in the chart pane, which means that Project has accepted your action. The task keeps the same duration.

- To print the milestones, use **View - Reports** and double-click first the **Overview** button then the **Milestones** button.
- Click the **Print** button in the preview that appears and confirm with **OK**. Click the **Close** button to close the **Reports** dialog box.
- To filter the milestones, open the **Filter** list.

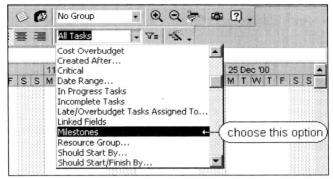

C-Assigning durations to tasks

Entering the duration

- Activate the duration cell.
- Enter just the number (if the duration already shows the correct unit) or follow the number with "m" for minutes, "h" for hours, "d" for days, "w" for weeks or "mo" for months then enter.
- To use elapsed duration and not working duration, use the codes "em" (elapsed minutes), "eh" (elapsed hours), "ed" (elapsed days), "ew" (elapsed weeks) or "emo" (elapsed months).

  Project sizes the bars in the Gantt Chart according to the durations entered.

⇨ *To change the default duration time units, use Tools - Options - Schedule tab. In the Duration is entered in list, choose the required time unit (changing this unit has no effect on the durations already entered).*

⇨ *To choose a duration display format, use Tools - Options - Edit tab and choose the required formats. If you do not want a space to appear between the numbers and the time units, deactivate the Add space before label option.*

D-Letting Project calculate the duration of a task

- Show the **PERT Analysis** toolbar using the **View - Toolbars - PERT Analysis** command.
- Click the ▦ (**PERT Entry Form**) tool button or the ▦ (**PERT Entry Sheet**) tool button.

The first tool displays a dialog box, the second a table called the **PA_PERT Entry Sheet.**

▨ For each task whose duration is to be analysed, enter its **Optimistic Duration**, its **Expected Duration** and its **Pessimistic Duration**.

▨ Click the ▨ tool button (**Calculate PERT**) to start the analysis.

⇨ *Project calculates a weighted average and displays the result in the **Duration** column.*

⇨ *To modify the weightings used by Project, click the* ▨ *tool button, set the new PERT weights (the sum of these must be 6) and confirm.*

⇨ *To show the Gantt Chart with the various durations, use these tools:* ▨ *(Optimistic Gantt),* ▨ *(Expected Gantt) or* ▨ *(Pessimistic Gantt).*

E-Setting up links between tasks

*A **Predecessor** is a task that must start or finish before another task can start. A **Successor** is a task that depends on the start or finish date of a previous task.*

A finish-to-start link between tasks

▨ In the **Gantt Sheet**, select the tasks that you want to link.

▨ Click the ▨ tool button or press ⌨Ctrl ⌨F2 .

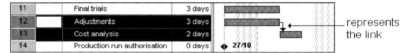

represents the link

Other types of link between two or more tasks

▨ Double-click a cell in the **Successor** task row.

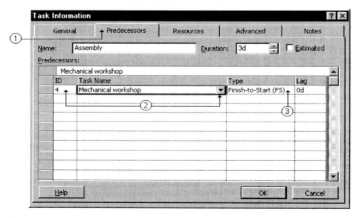

① Activate this tab.

② Type the predecessor task's number and press ⏎ or select the task in the drop-down list and confirm with ☑.

③ If the link suggested is incorrect, click this cell: open the proposed list and click the correct type of link.

▓ Establish all the links between this successor and its predecessors in the same way and click **OK**.

Other types of link between tasks (alternative method)

▓ In the Gantt Sheet, click the **Predecessor** cell of the successor task.

▓ Enter the predecessor task numbers, using the following rules:

Predecessor number(s):	
Only one predecessor:	enter its task number
Several predecessors:	enter the numbers, separating them with commas
Type of link:	
Finish-to-Start link:	enter only the numbers
Start-to-Start link:	suffix the number by the letters SS
Finish-to-Finish link:	suffix the number by the letters FF
Start-to-Finish link:	suffix the number by the letters SF

⇨ *To unlink a successor from all its predecessors, select the successor task and click the* ▓ *tool button or use* Ctrl ⇧ Shift F2 *.*

F-Specifying lag and lead times for links

Using the Task Information dialog box

▓ Double-click the successor task.

▓ Activate the **Predecessors** tab.

▓ Click in the **Lag** cell for the link concerned, enter the lag time using a positive value or the lead time with a negative value.

▓ Click **OK**.

⇨ *Lag and lead times can be expressed in working or elapsed time units (minutes, hours, days, months, weeks) or as percentages.*

Using the Entry Table

▓ Activate the **Predecessor** cell of the successor task.

▓ Follow the rules outlined above: but remember that for Finish-to-Start links, the letters FS **must** be entered when you specify lag or lead times.

▓ Enter the duration of the lag or lead time: use + (plus) for a lag time and -(minus) for a lead time.

TASKS

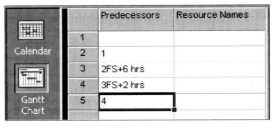

▓ Confirm your entry.

7.2 Managing tasks

A-Modifying the list of tasks

Deleting a task

▓ Click a cell on the row of the task that you want to delete.

▓ **Edit - Delete Task** or `Del`

Inserting a new task

▓ Click a cell in the task that will come after the new one.

▓ **Insert - New Task** or `Ins`

▓ Enter the data for the new task.

Copying a task

▓ Select the task that you want to copy by clicking its number.

▓ **Edit**   **C**
   Copy Task

▓ Select the destination row for the copy.

▓ **Edit**   **V**
   Paste

Moving a task

▓ Select the task row that you want to move.

▓ Point to the border of the row until the pointer appears as an arrow pointing upwards and to the left.

▓ Drag the row to its new position using the grey horizontal bar that appears as a guide.

⇨ *When you make changes, the tasks are renumbered.*

⇨ *If you are unable to use this technique, use* **Tools - Options - Edit** *tab, and activate the* **Allow cell drag and drop** *option.*

⇨ *When you carry out these different modifications, Project 2000 will normally attempt to update the links. If it does not do so, use* **Tools - Options - Schedule** *tab, and activate the* **Autolink inserted or moved tasks** *option: deactivate this if you want to manage the links yourself.*

B-Sorting the list of tasks

▓ **Project - Sort**

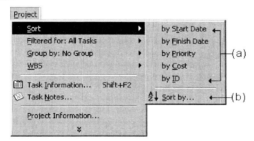

▓ Choose:

(a)   to sort using a standard criterion.

(b)   to sort using more advanced criteria:

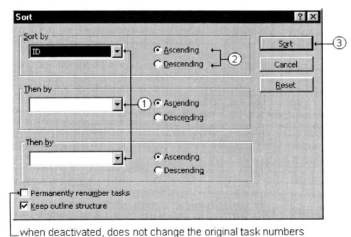

①When setting each sort criterion, select the field name in the appropriate list.

②Indicate the sort order.

③Start reorganising the tasks.

⇨ *If you did not ask to renumber the tasks, you can restore the tasks to their original order with* **Project - Sort - by ID** *or* ⬚ Shift ⬚ F3 ⬚.

C-Outlining the task list

*You can group tasks, known as **subtasks** into more general sets called **summary tasks**. This is referred to as outlining.*

▓ Create the summary task: immediately below it, list its subtasks, without any other tasks occurring between them.

▓ Drag to select the subtasks.

▓ Click the **Indent** tool button � or use ⟦Alt⟧⟦⇧ Shift⟧ ⟦→⟧.

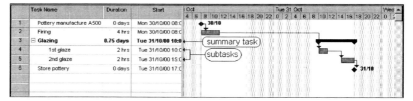

▓ To move a task up one level, click the task concerned and click the **Outdent** tool button ⬅ or use ⟦Alt⟧⟦⇧ Shift⟧ ⟦←⟧.

▓ To hide subtasks, select the summary task concerned and click the ▬ tool button or click the minus sign (-) that precedes the summary task name.

▓ To show the subtasks again, click the summary task and click the ✚ tool button or click the plus sign (+) that precedes the name of the summary task.

▓ To go to a specific outline level, open the **Show** drop-down list on the **Formatting** toolbar and choose the required outline level.

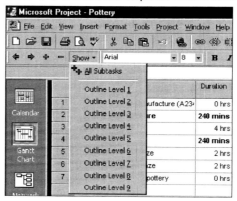

▓ To move a set of tasks in the outline, collapse the summary task containing the subtasks you want to move then move the summary task.

⇨ *Only the name of a summary task can be modified: all the rest is calculated by Project.*

⇨ *Project will allow you to insert a summary task into another summary task, providing you do not exceed 10 levels.*

D-Rolling up a Gantt bar into a summary

▒ Show the Gantt Chart.
▒ Double-click the subtask you wish to roll up.
▒ Click the **General** tab.
▒ Tick the **Roll up Gantt bar to summary** option then click **OK**.

E-Setting outline display options

▒ **Tools - Options - View** tab

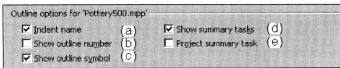

▒ Use the following options:

(a)   when this option is active, the subtasks appear indented.

(b)   if you tick this option, Project 2000 shows the outline number to the left of the **Task Name**.

(c)   when this option is active, Project shows outline symbols next to each summary task name.

(d)   if you deactivate this option, subtasks are hidden and you cannot use the outlining commands.

(e)   tick this option if you want to display a project level summary task. This will have an ID of 0.

F-Printing the tasks in an outline

▒ **View - Reports**
▒ Double-click the **Overview** option then double-click **Top-Level Tasks**.
▒ Click **Print** then **OK**.

G-Filtering the tasks in an outline

▒ Open the **Filter** list.

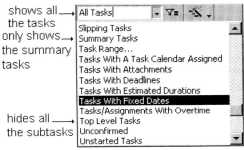

shows all → All Tasks
the tasks
only shows → Summary Tasks
the summary
tasks

hides all → Top Level Tasks
the subtasks

H-Setting a constraint date

▓ Double-click the task concerned.

▓ Activate the **Advanced** tab.

▓ Choose how you want to **Constrain** the **task** using:

As Late As Possible	The task must finish as late as possible according to the other constraints and links.
As Soon As Possible	This is equivalent to applying no constraint at all. The task will start as soon as possible according to the other constraints and links.
Finish No Earlier Than	The task must finish on the date you specify, at the earliest. Use this to ensure that a task will not finish before a specific date.
Finish No Later Than	The task must finish on the date you specify, at the latest. Use this to ensure that a task will not finish after a specific date.
Must Finish On [1]	The task must finish on a specific date.
Must Start On [1]	The task must start on a specific date.
Start No Earlier Than	The task must start on the date you specify, at the earliest. Use this to ensure that a task will not start before a specific date.
Start No Later Than	The task must start on the date you specify, at the latest. Use this to ensure that a task will not start after a specific date.

[1] *These are **inflexible** constraints: they leave no flexibility in the timing of the tasks concerned.*

▓ Give the **Constraint date**. As well as the date, you can specify the time, after having inserted a space (for example: 21/12/00 17:00).

▓ Click **OK**.

➭ *The* **▦** *indicator represents Finish No Earlier Than, Finish No Later Than, Start No Earlier Than and Start No Later Than constraints.*

➭ *The* **▦** *indicator represents Finish No Earlier Than, Finish No Later Than, Start No Earlier Than and Start No Later Than constraints.*

I- Entering notes on a task

Select the task for which you want to enter notes.

Click the 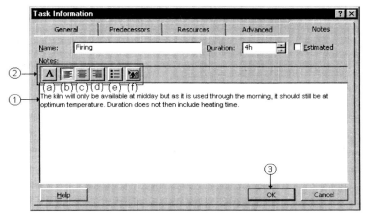 tool button or use **Project - Task Notes**.

① Enter your comments, using `Enter` to make a new paragraph or `⇧ Shift` `Enter` to make a line break.

② Change your note's presentation using these tool buttons:

(a)   to format the selected characters.

(b)   to left-align the selected paragraphs.

(c)   to centre the selected paragraphs.

(d)   to right-align the selected paragraphs.

(e)   to present the selected paragraphs as a bulleted list.

(f)   to insert an OLE object.

③ Confirm your note.

When a task contains a note, a note icon appears in the indicators column. If you point to this, the note's contents appear in a ScreenTip.

To open a note, select the task and click the tool button (or point to its icon in the indicators column to read the ScreenTip).

To filter annotated tasks, open the **Filter** list and select **Tasks With Attachments**.

J- Splitting a task

Show the Gantt Chart.

Click the tool button.

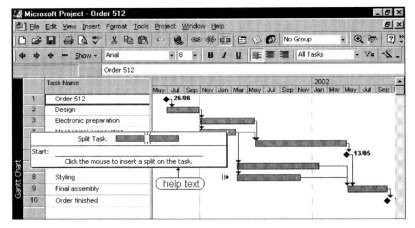

On the task bar, point to the place where you want to split the bar and drag to the right.

⇨ *As you drag, Project proposes dates linked to the minor timescale defined with* ***Format - Timescale***.

K-Creating recurring tasks

▓ Go to the place where the recurring task should appear.

▓ **Insert - Recurring Task**

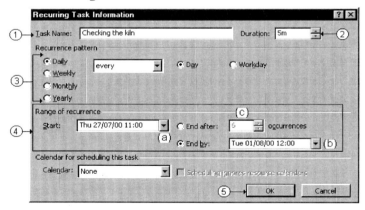

① Enter the task's name.

② Give its duration.

③ Specify how frequently it will occur.

④ To limit the task recurrence, use these options:
  to limit the recurrence in time, enter a start date in box (a) and an end date in box (b).
  to limit to a number of occurrences, enter this number in box (c).

⑤ Confirm.

⇨ *The task appears in the entry table as a summary task. It has this indicator:* ↻ *. One subtask is created for each occurrence of the task; each subtask takes the summary task's name, followed by a number.*

⇨ *Project creates these tasks at specific times. If changes are made to the project duration, the recurring tasks are not affected.*

⇨ *All of these tasks have a constraint date.*

L-Filtering tasks on a date range

▓ Open the **Filter** list and choose the **Date Range** option.
▓ Enter the earlier date in the range and click **OK**.
▓ Enter the later date in the range and click **OK**.

M-Setting an Outlook reminder for a task

▓ If you want Outlook to remind you of an upcoming task, show the project in the Gantt chart then click the task(s) for which you wish to receive a reminder.
▓ Click the **Set Reminder** 🔔 tool button on the **Workgroup** toolbar (**View - Toolbars - Workgroup**).
▓ Set the various options in the **Set Reminder** dialog box and click **OK**.

7.3 Optimising a project

TASKS

Optimising a project involves adjusting the critical path to meet deadlines and fine-tune task durations without compromising quality standards.

A-Adjusting the critical path

*The project finish date is directly related to the durations of the tasks on the critical path; this is why these tasks are called **critical tasks**. To optimise the overall project duration, you must first optimise the critical tasks.*

▓ Display the critical path by using **View - Gantt Chart**.

▓ Customise the Gantt chart shown by clicking the 🖾 tool button.

▓ Click the **Next** button to go to step 2.

▓ Choose the **Critical path** option and click **Finish**.

▓ Click the **Format It** button, then click **Exit Wizard**.

⇨ *The critical task bars and their links appear in red.*

⇨ *To display the critical path as a Network Diagram (or PERT chart), use* **View - Network Diagram (or PERT Chart)** *or click the* 🗗 *tool button. Critical tasks are shown in red boxes.*

B-Printing critical tasks

▓ In the Gantt Chart, filter the Critical tasks, display the columns that you require and start printing.
or
Display the **Network Diagram** and print it,
or
Use **View - Reports**.
Double-click the **Overview** button, then **Critical Tasks**.
Click the **Print** button, then **OK**.

⇨ *To filter critical tasks, open the* **Filter** *list and choose* **Critical**.

C-Setting critical task options

▓ **Tools - Options - Calculation** tab

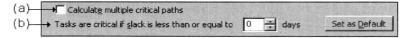

(a)——► ☐ Calculate multiple critical paths
(b)——► Tasks are critical if slack is less than or equal to ⬚ 0 ⬚ days   Set as Default

▓ Choose:

(a)   to display a critical path for each independent task network.

(b)   to set a different critical task definition threshold (other than 0).

D-Checking the validity of constraint dates

Using a filter

▓ Open the **Filter** list and click **Tasks With Fixed Dates**.

Project 2000 lists those tasks that have another constraint than **As soon as possible**. *However, you cannot view these constraint dates.*

As your project tracking progresses, this filter will also show tasks that have a real start date.

Using the Constraint Dates table

▓ **View - Table - More Tables**

▓ Double-click the **Constraint Dates** option.

	Duration	Constraint Type	Constraint Date
1	0 days	As Soon As Possible	NA
2	**25 days**	**As Soon As Possible**	**NA**
3	3 wks	As Soon As Possible	NA
4	9.5 days	As Soon As Possible	NA
5	0.5 days	As Soon As Possible	NA
6	0 days	As Soon As Possible	NA
7	**1.94 days**	**As Soon As Possible**	**NA**
8	5 hrs	Must Start On	Fri 29/09/00 13:00
9	12 hrs	As Soon As Possible	NA
10	12 hrs	Must Start On	Sun 01/10/00 08:00
11	5 hrs	As Soon As Possible	NA

⇨ *For each task, this table lists a number, the task name, its duration, its* **Constraint Type** *and the* **Constraint Date**.

E-Optimising links

Displaying the Predecessors & Successors form

▦ Display the Gantt Chart.

▦ **Window - Split**

▦ Right-click the form that appears and choose **Predecessors & Successors**.

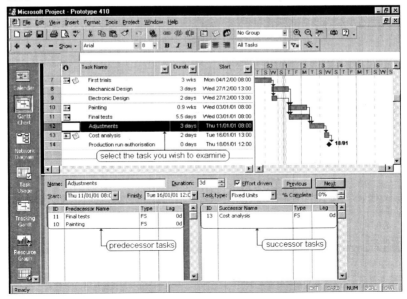

▦ Close the form and return to the original view with **Window - Remove Split**.

Displaying the Network Diagram

▦ Show the Gantt Chart.

▦ **Window - Split**

▦ Click the form to activate that part of the window.

▦ **View - More Views** or

▦ Double-click the **Network Diagram** (or **PERT Chart**) option.

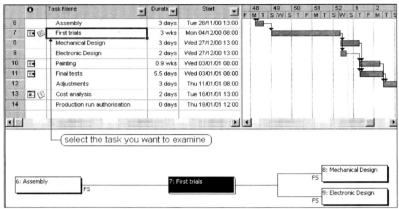

▦ Close this view with **Window - Remove Split**.

Creating a links table

▦ **View - Table - More Tables**

▦ Click the **New** button.

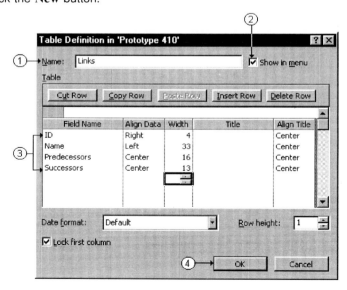

① Enter the name of the table.

② If required, activate this option to find your table more easily.

③ Insert at least the fields shown on this screen.

④ Click to confirm.

▓ Choose to **Apply** this table.

⇨ *Your new table replaces the Gantt Sheet: it exists only in the current project.*

⇨ *A few optimisation techniques:*

- *Try to find tasks that can run simultaneously. In practice, you can often convert Finish-to-Start links to Start-to-Start links with a lag, or leave them as Finish-to-Start types, but with a lead.*

- *See if you can break long tasks down into smaller tasks with their own links.*

F-Checking the slack

Using the Schedule table

▓ **View - Table - Schedule**

The two last columns of this table show **Free Slack** *and* **Total Slack**.

Using the Detail Gantt

▓ **View - More Views** or [image]

▓ Double-click the **Detail Gantt** option.

The critical task bars appear in red. The non-critical tasks appear in blue: their total slack is represented by green lines, and their free slack durations are displayed in figures. The **Delay** *table appears in this view.*

▓ If you cannot see the Gantt Chart, use **View - Zoom - Entire project - OK**.

8.1 Defining resources

*The tasks of a project are carried out using **Resources**. There are two types of resource: **Work** resources and **Material** resources. You can assign a resource to one or more tasks.*

***Work** resources are resources such as people and equipment, which devote time to the tasks that they carry out. **Material** resources are consumable stocks that are used by the project to carry out tasks.*

Resources have limited availability; you can share them between different projects. They have their own production capacities and they have associated costs.

***Material** resources do not use resource calendars and you cannot level them.*

A-Creating the resource list

▨ **View - Resource Sheet** or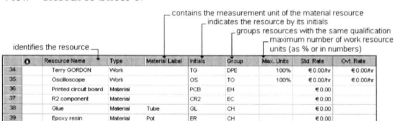

Labels pointing to the table:
- contains the measurement unit of the material resource
- indicates the resource by its initials
- groups resources with the same qualification
- maximum number of work resource units (as % or in numbers)
- identifies the resource

	●	Resource Name	Type	Material Label	Initials	Group	Max. Units	Std. Rate	Ovt. Rate
34		Terry GORDON	Work		TG	DPE	100%	€ 0.00/hr	€ 0.00/hr
35		Oscilloscope	Work		OS	TO	100%	€ 0.00/hr	€ 0.00/hr
36		Printed circuit board	Material		PCB	EH		€ 0.00	
37		R2 component	Material		CR2	EC		€ 0.00	
38		Glue	Material	Tube	GL	CH		€ 0.00	
39		Epoxy resin	Material	Pot	ER	CH		€ 0.00	

▨ For each work resource, specify the **Resource Name**, the **Type**, the **Initials**, the **Group** and the **Max. Units**.

▨ For each material resource, enter a **Resource Name**, its **Type**, its **Material Label**, its **Initials** and its **Group**.

⇨ *To insert a resource into the list, click the row where it should appear and press the* [Ins] *key or use **Insert - New Resource**.*

⇨ *You can enter any type of measurement unit as the **Material Label**, such as tonnes, m (for metres), box, pot and so on.*

⇨ *To delete a resource, click the resource concerned and press the* [Del] *key or use **Edit - Delete Resource**.*

B-Defining maximum units for a work resource

▨ In the resource sheet, click the **Max. Units** field for the resource concerned.

▨ Indicate how much time the resource must devote to the project. For example: 100% for full time, 50% for half time, or 300% for "multiple time" (the resource could correspond to three people working full time on the project).

The time specified at this level concerns the project as a whole. Do not confuse this with the time that you indicate when you assign a resource to a task. Unlike the maximum work capacity, each assignment unit indicates the amount of time that the resource can devote to a specific task.

You must define the maximum number of units for each resource or for each set of consolidated resources. Project 2000 makes no tests or checks at this level. However, Project does compare the maximum number of units with the number of units assigned to task(s) to determine whether or not the resource is overallocated.

⇨ *To present the maximum number of units as a percentage or a decimal number, use* **Tools - Options - Schedule** *tab. Choose* **Percentage** *or* **Decimal** *in the* **Show assignment units as a** *box.*

C-Sorting the resource list

▨ **Project - Sort**

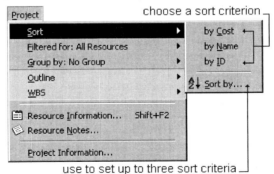

⇨ *As with task sorts, if you did not ask Project to renumber resources you can cancel the sort with* ⎣0 Shift⎦ ⎣F3⎦ .

RESOURCES

D-Adapting the calendar to a work resource

▓ **Tools - Change Working Time**

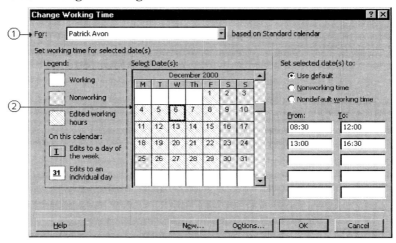

① Click the name of the resource concerned.

② Adapt the calendar to the resource's needs.

⇨ *If you want a hard copy of the created calendars, proceed as if you were printing the project calendar.*

E-Managing a calendar for several resources

▓ To create a new calendar, use the **Tools - Change Working Time** command and click the **New** button.

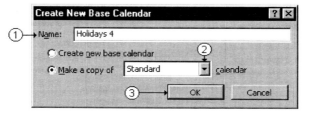

① Give the new calendar a name.

② Choose the calendar of which you want to make a copy.

③ Confirm.

▓ Adapt the calendar to your needs then click **OK** to create it.

▓ To apply the calendar to the resources concerned, activate the **Base Calendar** cell for the resource and open the drop-down list.

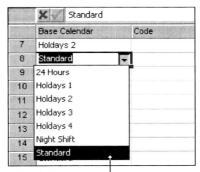

click the right calendar⎦
for the resource

F- Entering a note on a resource

▦ To create the note, select the resource concerned. Click the 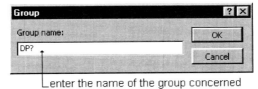 tool button and enter your remarks. If required, format your note and click **OK**.

As with tasks, a note icon appears in the indicators column for resources with notes attached.

▦ To edit a note, double-click the icon shown in the indicators column and make your changes then click **OK**.

▦ To consult a specific note, point to the note icon in the indicators column. To consult several notes, use **Window - Split**. Right-click the displayed form and choose **Notes**. In the top part of the window, select the re-source in question. To close this view, use **Window - Remove Split**.

⇨ *To filter resources with notes attached, open the* ***Filter*** *list and click* ***Re-sources With Attachments***.

G-Filtering resources for a specific group

▦ Display the resource sheet.

▦ Open the **Filter** list and click the **Group** option.

⎣enter the name of the group concerned

⇨ *For text type fields you can use the wildcard characters ? and *.*

RESOURCES

H-Printing the resource list

▦ Show the resource sheet.

▦ Use to open a print preview.

▦ To change page orientation, click the **Page Setup** button, activate the **Page** tab and click the **Landscape** option. Confirm with **OK**.

▦ Click the **Print** button then **OK**.

8.2 Assigning resources

A-Looking at effort driven scheduling

▦ Microsoft Project 2000 reduces or increases the duration of a task according to changes in the resources assigned, but it does not change the total work for the task. Remember that the total work is different from a task's duration. The total work for a task is the number of working hours required for all the resources to complete that task.

▦ As you assign resources to a task, be aware that the total work for the task stays the same. On the other hand, the amount of work distributed amongst the resources assigned to this task does change. This process, used by default in Project 2000, is called **effort driven scheduling**.

▦ You can deactivate this process, which may be useful, for example, when you want to increase the total work for a specific task as you assign resources to it.
When the effort driven option is set, the calculations that can change the duration of the task are applied only after a first assignment of one or more resources to the task.

⇨ *To deactivate effort-driven scheduling for all the new tasks created, use* ***Tools - Options - Schedule*** *tab and deactivate the* ***New tasks are effort driven*** *option.*

B-Assigning resources to one or more tasks

▦ Show the Gantt Chart.

▦ Select all the tasks to which you want to assign the same resources and click the ⬛ tool button.

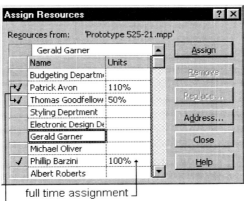

full time assignment
represent assigned resources

▓ To assign a resource full time, select it then click the **Assign** button.

To assign several units of the same resource, enter a percentage greater than 100 or the number of units you want to assign.

To assign a resource part time, enter a decimal value or a percentage less than 100.

⇨ *The resource names appear in the Gantt Chart and also in the final column of the task sheet.*

⇨ *Depending on the calendars of the assigned resources, the task duration may be modified.*

⇨ *The first time you assign a resource to a task, Project does not vary the task duration, even if the Effort driven option is active.*

C-Delaying the work of a resource on a task

▓ Go to the **Resource Schedule** form for the task concerned.

▓ Work in the **Delay** column of the resource concerned then click **OK**.

⇨ *If the Effort driven option is active, the task duration increases and the next task is delayed.*

D-Defining a work contour

When you assign a resource to a task, Project automatically allocates the same number of hours per time period, for the whole duration of the task.

▓ **View - Task Usage** or 🔲

▓ To choose a predefined work contour, double-click the resource concerned in the task in question. Open the **Work contour** list under the **General** tab and choose the required contour. Click **OK**.

▓ To customise a contour, click the resource concerned then click the 🖉 tool to go to the task. Enter, for each day, the hours the resource devotes to that task.

⇨ *An icon appears in the indicators column, representing the chosen contour:*

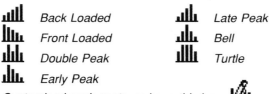

⣿	Back Loaded	⣿	Late Peak
⣿	Front Loaded	⣿	Bell
⣿	Double Peak	⣿	Turtle
⣿	Early Peak		

⇨ *Customised work contours have this icon:* ⣿.

E-Displaying resource initials in the Gantt Chart

▓ Show the Gantt Chart concerned.

▓ **Format - Bar Styles**

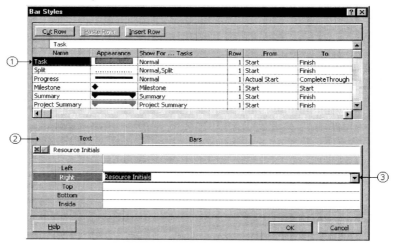

① Select this cell.

② Activate this tab.

③ Open this list then select the **Resource Initials** option.

⇨ *The information on the number of units assigned disappears.*

F-Printing resource assignments

▓ **View - Reports**

▓ Double-click the **Assignments** button.

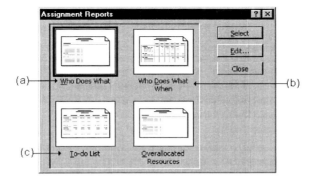

■ Choose:

(a) or (b)	to print the assignments for all resources.
(c)	to print the assignments for a resource (you will have to give its name).

⇨ *You can also filter a resource's assignments. To do this, show the tasks, open the* **Filter** *list and click* **Using Resource** *or* **Using Resource in Date Range**.

G-Changing a resource assignment

■ Double-click the task for which you want to modify the resource assignment.

■ Activate the **Advanced** tab.

■ If the assignment changes are not to affect the task duration, deactivate the **Effort driven** option.
If your changes should affect the duration, make sure this option is active.

■ When effort-driven scheduling is active, the option that is selected in the **Task type** box in the **Task Information** dialog box may affect the recalculation of the task duration.

■ Click **OK**.

■ Open the **Assign Resources** dialog box.

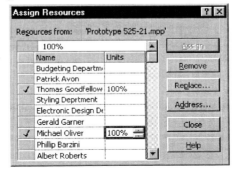

- To add a resource, proceed as you would for an initial resource assignment.
- To remove a resource assignment, select the resource concerned and click the **Remove** button.
- To replace a resource, select the resource you want to replace and click the **Replace** button; choose the new resource and confirm.
- To change the number of units assigned, changing the task duration, proceed as for an initial assignment.
- To modify the number of units assigned, without changing the task duration, go to the **Task Information** dialog box, deactivate the **Effort driven** option and make sure the **Task type** is **Fixed Duration**. Next, click the **Replace** button in the **Assign Resources** dialog box and enter in the **Units** cell of the resource the correct number of units or percentage.

8.3 Optimising assignments

A-Displaying resource assignments

- **View - Resource Usage** or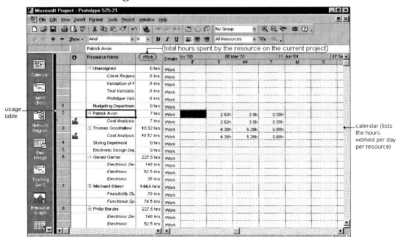

⇨ *The Gantt Chart shows the name of assigned resources and the number of units. The **Entry Table** also displays this information in its final column. The **Resource Work** form provides information concerning overtime hours and the **Resource Schedule** form shows any delays.*

B-Modifying the Resource Usage view

▨ To change the timescale, use **Format - Timescale**. Make your customisations and confirm.

▨ To choose which information will be displayed in the calendar, right-click the calendar pane of the **Resource Usage** view.

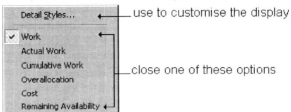

use to customise the display

close one of these options

▨ To show the resource allocation, display the **Resource Sheet** or the **Resource Usage** view then activate the **View - More Views** command or

 and double-click the **Resource Allocation** option.

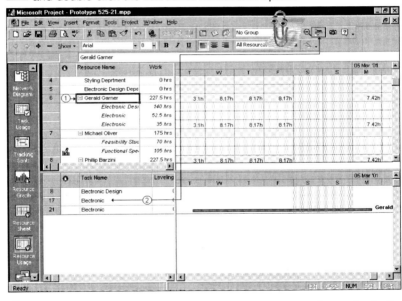

① Click the resource you wish to study (you can see the tasks in the lower section).

② To show the bar relating to one of the resource's tasks, click the task and use the tool button.

▨ Leave this view with **Window - Remove Split**.

▨ To display the task usage, choose **View - Task Usage** or .

RESOURCES

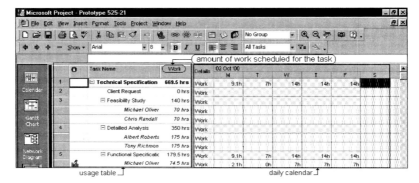

⇨ *If you cannot see the names of the resources assigned to a task, click that task then the* 🔧 *tool button.*

C-Authorising overtime work

▪ Select the task concerned.

▪ **Window - Split**

▪ Right-click the form that appears and choose **Resource Work**.

▪ In the **Ovt. Work** column, enter the overtime authorised, following these guidelines:
If the task duration should decrease accordingly, enter just the number of overtime hours.
If the task duration should remain unchanged, give the number of overtime hours and the number of work hours. This calculation will be made:
DURATION (of task) = WORK - OVERTIME.

▪ Confirm by clicking **OK** in the form.

▪ To return to a normal view, use **Window - Remove Split**.

⇨ *To filter tasks that have overtime assigned, open the Filter list and click Tasks/Assignments With Overtime.*

⇨ *When the Previous and Next buttons replace the OK button, you know Project has accepted your changes.*

D-Displaying the Summary table for resources

▪ Go into **Resource Usage** or **Resource Sheet** view.

▪ **View - Table - Summary**

maximum number of units assigned
to the resource at a given time

	Resource Name	Group	Max. Units	Peak	Std. Rate	Ovt. Rate	Cost	Work
1	Budgeting Departmen	DB	200%	0%	€ 0.00/hr	€ 0.00/hr	€ 0.00	0 h
2	Patrick Avon	DB	100%	50%	€ 0.00/hr	€ 0.00/hr	€ 0.00	7 h
3	Thomas Goodfellow	DB	100%	70%	€ 0.00/hr	€ 0.00/hr	€ 0.00	9.8 h
4	Styling Deprtment	DE	800%	0%	€ 0.00/hr	€ 0.00/hr	€ 0.00	0 h

E- Studying overallocated resources

A resource is overallocated when the work you assign to that resource exceeds its available work.

- In the **Resource Sheet, Resource Allocation** and **Resource Usage** views, overallocated resources appear in red.

- In **Resource Allocation** view, the ⬧ indicator precedes all overallocated resources.

- To see only the overallocated resources, open the **Filter** list and click **Overallocated Resources**.

- To print them, use **View - Reports** and double-click **Assignments** then **Overallocated Resources**. Choose **Print - OK** and click **Close** to leave the dialog box.

- To display the overallocated work hours, go into **Resource Usage** view. Right-click the calendar pane and choose the **Overallocation** option. Move over the time period you want to examine.

F- Solving overallocation problems by levelling

With levelling, Project 2000 delays or splits certain tasks so assigned resources are no longer overallocated.

- Go to resource levelling using **Tools - Resource Leveling**.

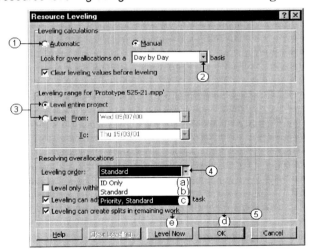

① Choose the appropriate option (it is preferable to choose **Manual**).

② Choose the time period over which Project 2000 should look for overallocations before making its levelling calculations.

③ Choose to **Level entire project** or level only the tasks in a specific time period by activating the **Level** option and giving the time period in the **From** and **To** boxes.

Microsoft Project 2000

RESOURCES

④ Set the **Leveling order**:
  - (a) Project starts by delaying the task with the highest ID number.
  - (b) Project studies links with predecessors, slack, dates and priorities to choose which task to delay.
  - (c) Project determines which task to delay by examining first the priorities, then the links with predecessors, the slack, and the dates.

⑤ Confirm the information given (d) or confirm and start the levelling (e).

▨ To define task priorities, select the tasks for which you want to assign the same priority level then click the 🖽 tool button.

▨ If necessary, activate the **General** tab.

▨ In the **Priority** field, indicate the importance of the tasks selected with a number between 0 and 1000 (the higher the number, the higher the priority for the task concerned).

*Nothing indicates the priorities that you have defined, but you can view these priority settings by inserting the **Priority** column into the table (use the **Insert - Column** command).*

▨ To see the delays in a Gantt view, use **View - More Views** then double-click **Leveling Gantt**. If necessary, zoom the view.

*This view displays the **Delay** table, which contains the **Leveling Delay** column. The Gantt Chart shows the delays with thin green lines.*

▨ To clear resource levelling, use **Tools - Resource Leveling** and click the **Clear Leveling** button then **OK**.

Project cancels all delays in the project.

⇨ *To display task or delay information in a ScreenTip, point to the corresponding line.*

⇨ *There are several ways of solving overallocation problems. You can:*

  - *delay a task by entering a suitable value into the **Leveling Delay** field for the task (access this field with **View - Table - More Tables - Delay**),*
  - *break long tasks down into subtasks to assign resources more precisely,*
  - *split tasks,*
  - *subcontract certain tasks (overallocation problems will no longer be your responsibility),*
  - *delay the work done by a resource using the **Delay** column of the **Resource Schedule** form,*
  - *adjust the resource calendars, authorising overtime work to increase resource availability,*
  - *assign new resources to reduce the duration of the tasks,*
  - *replace resources by other resources that have more availibility,*
  - *optimise resource usage.*

9.1 Costs

Cost considerations can affect how quickly you carry out tasks and how you use resources. Comparing the costs at the end of a project with the planned costs is a way of measuring the success of your project. Project 2000 can manage task costs and resource costs.

A-Entering task costs

▓ Show the tasks in the Gantt Chart.

▓ **View - Table - Cost**

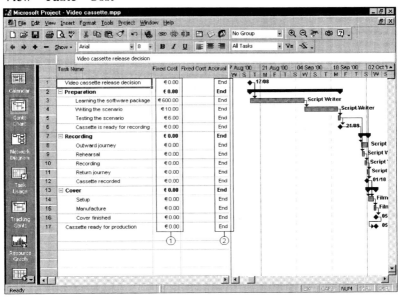

① Enter the task costs.

② Choose when and how you want the cost to be attributed to, or incurred by, the tasks: **Start**, **Prorated** or **End**.

⇨ *The **Total Cost** calculated field summarises the fixed costs for tasks and the costs of their assigned resources.*

B-Entering costs for work resources

▨ Display the resource sheet with its entry table.

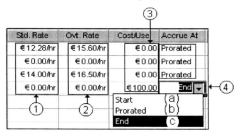

① Enter the basic hourly rate.

② Give the hourly overtime cost for the resource.

③ Enter the fixed usage cost for the resource. This sum is added each time a unit of this resource is assigned to a task. It is a fixed sum, irrespective of the length of time the resource is in use.

④ Specify the method for incurring the cost:

    (a)   The resource cost is incurred when the task starts.

    (b)   The cost will be incurred incrementally, as the task progresses.

    (c)   The cost is incurred when the remaining work is equal to zero.

⇨ *By default, Project assigns resource costs of zero. If your project uses standard rates, specify it using **Tools - Options - General** tab. Give the hourly **Default standard rate** and the **Default overtime rate**. These rates apply only to new resources that you create.*

⇨ *The **Standard Rate** field corresponds to the resource's wage rate.*

C-Entering costs for material resources

▨ Display the resource table.

▨ Select the resource concerned.

	Material Label	Initials	Group	Max Units	Std. Rate	Ovt. Rate	Cost/Use	Accr
1		SE	Training	100%	€ 12.28/hr	€ 15.60/hr	€ 0.00	Prora
2		FCR	Video	100%	€ 0.00/hr	€ 0.00/hr	€ 0.00	Prora
3		FCU	Film cutters	400%	€ 14.00/hr	€ 16.50/hr	€ 0.00	Prora
4		PS	Subcontractors	100%	€ 0.00/hr	€ 0.00/hr	€ 100.00	End
5	Litre	LPG	Fuel		€ 1.00		€ 0.00	Prora
6		CM	Cover		(a) € 0.00		(b) € 50.00	Prora

① If necessary, give the measurement unit used by that material resource.

② Enter the unit price for the resource (a) or the usage cost that will be billed to the task linked to that resource (b).

⇨ *To insert the **Standard Rate** field in the table, use **Insert - Column**.*

D-Assigning new cost rates to resources

▦ Double-click the resource for which a future increase (or decrease) in salary is planned.

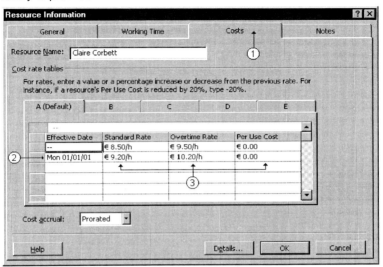

① Activate this tab.

② Give the date when the rate changes will become effective.

③ Enter the new rate or a percentage increase (or decrease). Once you enter the percentage, Project calculates the new rate.

⇨ *The first row should not be changed.*

E-Using several cost rate tables for a resource

▦ To create a table, double-click the resource concerned and activate the **Costs** tab. Click the tab of the cost rate table on which you want to work: **A (Default), B, C, D** or **E**. Enter the different costs in the chosen table and confirm.

▦ To choose a particular cost rate table, use **View - Resource Usage** or
▦. Double-click the assignment for which you want to specify a different cost rate table.

▦ In the drop-down list on the **Cost rate table** field, select the name of the table Project should use.

⇨ *To delete a value in one of the fields of a Cost rate table, replace the value by zero.*

F-Filtering tasks with costs exceeding a certain value

▓ Display the tasks.

▓ Open the **Filter** list and select the **Cost Greater Than** filter.

▓ Enter the reference value and confirm.

G-Printing the Cash Flow report

*This report presents the costs per task and per week, the total costs of all tasks per week, the total costs per task (this equals the **Total Cost** field in the task sheet) and the total budget cost. Project uses the total cost of each task, it divides this by the total duration of the task, and it multiplies the result by the duration of the task in each week.*

▓ **View - Reports**

▓ Double-click the **Costs** button, then **Cash flow**.

▓ Choose to **Print** then click **OK**.

▓ Leave the dialog box by clicking the **Close** button.

H-Viewing the cost accumulation of a resource

Using a graph

▓ **View - Resource Graph** or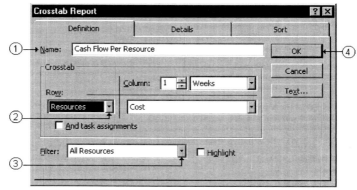

▓ Right-click the right pane of the screen and choose **Cumulative Cost**.

Using a custom cash flow report

▓ **View - Reports**

▓ Double-click the **Custom** button.

▓ Choose **Cash Flow** in the list and click the **Copy** button.

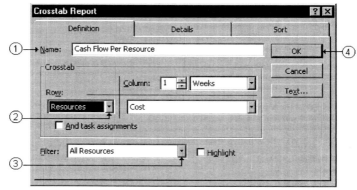

① Enter the name of the new report.

② Select the **Resources** option in this list.

③ Choose the **All Resources** option in this list.

④ Enter.

░ To use your custom cash flow report, select it in the **Reports** list and choose to **Print** or **Preview** it.

I- Looking at the Earned Value table

░ To display the Earned Value table, use 0**View - Tables - More Tables**. Double-click the **Earned Value** option.

░ To print the Earned Value table, use **View - Reports**. Double-click **Costs**, then **Earned Value**.

⇨ *You can show just the table in the view with View - More Views - Task Table - Apply.*

J- Studying the columns in the Earned Value table

Task Name	BCWS	BCWP	ACWP	SV	CV	EAC	BAC	VAC
1	Video cassette releas	€ 0.00	€ 0.00	€ 0.00	€ 0.00	€ 0.00	€ 0.00	€ 0.00	€ 0.00
2	⊟ Preparation	€ 1,512.00	€ 1,377.60	€ 125.90	-€ 134.40	€ 1,251.70	€ 6,444.00	€ 6,444.00	€ 0.00
3	Learning the soft	€ 1,512.00	€ 1,377.60	€ 125.90	-€ 134.40	€ 1,251.70	€ 1,680.00	€ 1,680.00	€ 0.00
4	Writing the scene	€ 0.00	€ 0.00	€ 0.00	€ 0.00	€ 0.00	€ 758.00	€ 758.00	€ 0.00
5	Tuning the scene	€ 0.00	€ 0.00	€ 0.00	€ 0.00	€ 0.00	€ 6.00	€ 6.00	€ 0.00
6	Cassette is read	€ 0.00	€ 0.00	€ 0.00	€ 0.00	€ 0.00	€ 4,000.00	€ 4,000.00	€ 0.00

░ The **EAC** (Estimate At Completion) column contains the total cost of each task. This corresponds to the **Total** column of the weekly cash flow report.

░ If you save the baseline for your project with **Tools - Tracking - Save Baseline - OK**, Project copies the **EAC** column into the **BAC** (Budget At Completion) column, which corresponds to the baseline cost.

░ The **BCWS** column shows the Budgeted Cost of Work Scheduled at a given date. This is the part of the budget that should have been used if the project had progressed according to the initial plan. **BCWS = BAC x % of planned completion.**

Project 2000 calculates using elapsed durations and not worked durations.

░ The **BCWP** column shows the Budgeted Cost of Work Performed (also known as "earned value").
BCWP = BAC x % actual completion.

░ The **ACWP** column shows the Actual Cost of Work Performed: it represents the real costs of the tasks.

░ The **SV** (earned value Schedule Variance) column shows, in cost terms, the difference between the current progress and the planned progress for the tasks.
SV = BCWP - BCWS

░ The **CV** (earned value Cost Variance) column shows the budget variation.
CV = ACWP - BCWP

░ The **VAC** (Variance At Completion) column shows the difference between the actual cost and the estimated cost (**VAC = BAC - EAC**).

K-Changing the currency format for costs

▓ **Tools - Options - View** tab

Currency options for 'Video Cassette Project'

Symbol:	€	Decimal digits:	2
Placement:	€ 1		

└change the options as required

9.2 Workload

A-Entering the workload on a task

▓ Show the Gantt Chart.

▓ **View - Table - Work**

	Task Name	Work	Baseline	Variance	Actual	Remaining	% W. Comp.
1	Order 512	0 hrs	0 hrs	0 hrs	0 hrs	0 hrs	0%
2	Specification	4 hrs	0 hrs	4 hrs	1 hr	3 hrs	25%
3	Design	0 hrs	0 hrs	0 hrs	0 hrs	0 hrs	0%
4	Electronic preparation	0 hrs	0 hrs	0 hrs	0 hrs	0 hrs	0%
5	Mechanical preparation	0 hrs	0 hrs	0 hrs	0 hrs	0 hrs	0%
6	Electronic and mechanical tests	0 hrs	0 hrs	0 hrs	0 hrs	0 hrs	0%
7	Tests validated	0 hrs	0 hrs	0 hrs	0 hrs	0 hrs	0%
8	Mechanical sub-assembly	0 hrs	0 hrs	0 hrs	0 hrs	0 hrs	0%
9	Styling	0 hrs	0 hrs	0 hrs	0 hrs	0 hrs	0%
10	Final assembly	0 hrs	0 hrs	0 hrs	0 hrs	0 hrs	0%
11	Order finished	0 hrs	0 hrs	0 hrs	0 hrs	0 hrs	0%

└enter the workloads

▓ If the time unit suggested in the **Work** column is unsuitable for your project, use **Tools - Options**, activate the **Schedule** tab, modify the option used in the **Work is entered in** list and click **OK**.

B-Printing the task workload

▓ **View - Reports**

▓ Double-click the **Workload** button then the **Task Usage** button.

▓ To print the report click **Print** then **OK**.

▓ To view the report on the screen, click anywhere in the table.

10.1 Project progress

A-Monitoring your project's progress

▓ Before you can start tracking your project, you must define a baseline for it.

▓ A project that manages only tasks is easy to track: you compare only the planned dates with the actual dates, and the differences in durations. With more sophisticated projects, tracking becomes more complex: comparing costs, numbers of hours worked and so on.

▓ Tracking allows you to spot variations, solve problems before they become critical and enhance your professional knowledge.

B-Saving the baseline

After you have set up your plan and before your project starts, you must define a baseline so you can track your project by comparing actual data with your planned data.
When you save the baseline, Project saves many items of information, including:

Data Item	Saved As
Duration	Baseline duration
Start	Baseline start
Finish	Baseline finish

You can resave your baseline as often as you like to reflect important changes. Project does not allow tracking until you have saved a baseline.

▓ **Tools - Tracking - Save Baseline**

▓ Keep the **Save baseline** and **Entire project** options active then enter.

⇨ *To clear the baseline, use **Tools - Tracking - Clear Baseline**, activate the **Clear baseline plan** option and click **OK**.*

C-Saving an interim plan

You can use this technique when your project is underway, after you have saved a baseline.

▓ **Tools - Tracking - Save Baseline**

Microsoft Project 2000

① Activate this option.

② Specify from which fields you want to copy.

③ Give the destination fields for the copy.

➡ *Project can save up to 10 different interim plans.*

➡ *To clear an interim plan, use **Tools - Tracking - Clear Baseline**. Activate the **Clear interim plan** option, open the corresponding list and select the interim plan that you want to clear. Click **OK**.*

D-Entering the current date of your project

▓ **Project - Project Information**

▓ Give the current date of your project in the **Current date** box and enter.

➡ *The current date (whether automatic or manually entered) appears in the Gantt Chart. The tasks to its left are in the past and should be completed, the tasks through which this line passes are in the present and should be underway, and those to the right of it are in the future and should not yet have started.*

➡ *Entering the current date for your project in this way is only a temporary setting. If you close your file and reopen it, Project reverts to the current date of your computer.*

E-Consulting the different plans

▓ **View - Table - More Tables**

▓ To show the table of scheduled tasks, double-click **Schedule**.

▓ To show another type of plan, click the **New** button.

▓ Enter a **Name**.

▓ Activate the **Show in menu** check box, if required.

▓ Insert your choice of columns.

▓ Click **OK** and choose to **Apply**.

F-Viewing the Progress Lines

For a given progress date, Project 2000 can draw a progress line through the tasks underway.

Tools - Tracking - Progress Lines - Dates and Intervals tab

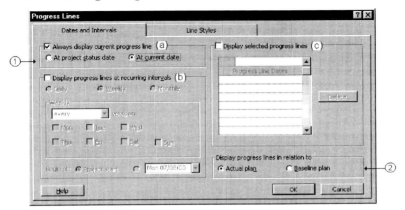

① Choose:

(a) to show the current progress line (**At project status date** or **At current date**).

(b) to show progress lines at regular intervals (specify the interval required).

(c) to display progress lines at specific dates (give the dates of your choice in the next column).

② Choose to show the progress line in relation to the actual plan or the baseline plan.

⇨ *The peaks pointing to the left indicate tasks that are running late and peaks pointing to the right represent tasks that are running ahead of schedule.*

If necessary, show the tracking toolbar with **View - Toolbars - Tracking**.

Click the ▦ tool button.

In the Gantt Chart, click where you wish the progress line to appear.

⇨ *A task is ahead of schedule when its actual start date is earlier than its planned start date.*

10.2 Tasks progress

A-Updating tasks progress

▨ **Tools - Tracking - Update Project**

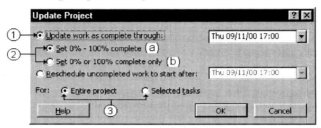

① Keep this option active and, if necessary, enter the update date in the text box.

② Choose:

(a) Project calculates real progress percentages.

(b) Projects assigns 100% to completed tasks and 0% for the others even if they are underway.

③ If necessary, indicate which tasks you wish to update.

⇨ *Black lines representing progress percentages appear in the Gantt Chart. The ✓ indicator shows that a task has been tracked.*

⇨ *You can also click the* ⊡ *(Update as Scheduled) tool button to let Project calculate the progress of all tasks.*

⇨ *You can also update tasks by entering your own information.*

B-Entering tracking information

▨ Select the task whose progress you want to update.

▨ **Tools - Tracking - Update Tasks** or ⊡

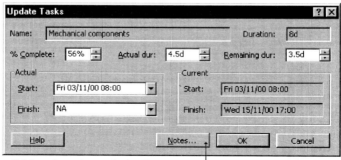

click to enter notes on the task's progress⌐

- For completed tasks, if all has gone according to plan, enter **100** in the **% Complete** box or **0** in the **Remaining dur** box. If the task took longer than planned, enter its actual duration in the corresponding box.

  Project considers a task to be completed when its actual duration is greater than or equal to the planned duration. It also considers a task to be completed if you specify its actual finish date

- To indicate that a task has not yet been completed, specify a **% Complete** value of between 0 and 100 or an **Actual dur** value less than the planned duration.

- If you enter information in only one of these boxes, Project will calculate the other data in relation to the baseline. If these calculations do not reflect reality, use more than one of these boxes. Be careful: Project does not take the current date into account when making these calculations.

C-Rescheduling slipped tasks

- Select the tasks concerned.
- **Tools - Tracking - Update Project**

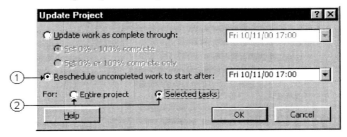

① Activate this option and, if necessary, fill in the date in the text box.

② Specify for which tasks the rescheduling applies.

⇨ *You can also use the* ⬛ *(Reschedule Work) tool button.*

D-Viewing the variance between your plan and reality

Using the Tracking Gantt

- **View - Tracking Gantt**
- If necessary, use **View - Zoom - Entire project - OK**.

  The grey layers of the task bars show what you scheduled. The blue layers (or the red layers for critical tasks) show the real situation. The completion percentages for the tasks also appear.

Using the Variance table

▓ **View - Table - Variance**

*The last columns of this table show the **Start Variance** and the **Finish Variance**.* Project transfers variances from one task to the next according to their scheduling.

Using a custom table

▓ **View - Table - More Tables**

▓ To define your custom table, click the **New** button.

▓ Fill in the **Table Definition** dialog box.

▓ Click **OK** then **Apply**.

▓ Use this table like any other.

E-Examining tasks

By applying a filter

▓ In a task view, open the **Filter** list.

▓ In the list, click **Completed Tasks**, **In Progress Tasks** or **Slipping Tasks**.

By printing a report

▓ **View - Reports** then double-click the **Current Activities** button.

▓ Once again, double-click **Completed Tasks, In Progress Tasks** or **Slipping Tasks**.

▓ Choose to **Print** and confirm with **OK**.

⇨ *The **Incomplete Tasks** filter displays all tasks that have not yet been completed, whether they have been started or not.*

10.3 Tracking resources

A-Tracking the work of each assigned resource

On completed tasks

▓ Show the **Task Usage** table.

▓ **Window - Split**

▓ Right-click the form that appears and choose the **Resource Work** form.

*When you save the baseline, Project copies the **Work** field into the **Baseline Work** field.*

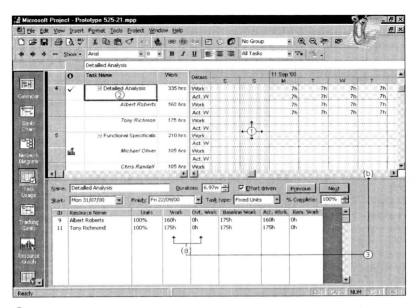

① Right-click this (yellow) pane and choose the **Actual Work** option.

② Select the task concerned.

③ If the **Actual Work** is greater than the **Baseline Work**, but the elapsed duration of the task has not been altered, indicate how this work was carried out:

(a)   If you used overtime, fill in the **Work** and **Ovt. Work** fields in the **Resource Work** form.

(b)   if the resource worked more hours without doing overtime, and these extra hours have a cost, enter the actual hours worked in the right pane of the **Task Usage** view for the resource concerned.

▓ If necessary, confirm with **OK**.

On tasks in progress

▓ Display the **Gantt Chart** view with the **Resource Work** form.

▓ When you track for the first time, enter the **Actual Work** in the **Resource Work** form in question.

▓ A problem arises when you update the tracking information: resources often report the work carried out since the last tracking. The initial solution might be to add this new value to the previous one. However, if you give a new progress percentage to the task, Project will instantly recalculate the actual work. How then can you find the previous actual work figure?

▓ To solve this problem in tracking updates, you should dissociate the task update from the resource update or update the actual work on a daily basis.

B-Dissociating task/resource updates

▓ **Tools - Options - Calculation** tab

deactivate
this option

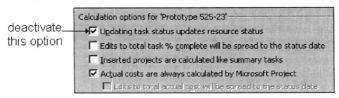

C-Updating actual work on a daily basis

▓ **View - Resource Usage** or

▓ **View - Table - Work**

▓ Enter the hours worked in the calendar pane of this view.

D-Showing the % work complete in the Tracking Gantt

▓ Show the **Tracking Gantt.**

▓ **Format - Bar Styles**

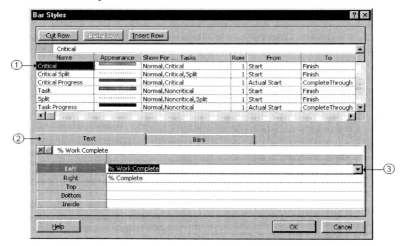

① Click this cell.

② Activate this tab.

③ Select the **% Work Complete** field in the list attached to this cell.

▓ Customise the non-critical bars in the same way then enter.

10.4 Tracking costs and overall work

A-Tracking actual costs

▨ To deactivate the automatic calculation of costs, use **Tools - Options - Calculation** tab. Deactivate the **Actual costs are always calculated by Microsoft Project** option. Activate the **Edits to total task % complete will be spread to the status date** option or deactivate it to spread cost modifications to the end of the actual duration of the task. Enter.

▨ To enter actual costs, display the tasks and use **View - Table - Cost**. Enter the actual costs in the **Actual** field.

B-Setting the status date

The status date of a project is used to calculate the values in the Earned Value table. If you do not specify this date, Project 2000 calculates these values according to the current date.

▨ **Project - Project Information**
▨ Enter the **Status date**.
▨ Confirm with **OK**.

C-Reviewing overbudget costs

On the screen

▨ Open the **Filter** list.
▨ Select **Cost Overbudget** or **Work Overbudget**.

By printing a report

▨ **View - Reports**
▨ Double-click the **Costs** button.
▨ Double-click **Overbudget Tasks** or **Overbudget Resources** then print the report.

D-Tracking overall work carried out on tasks

▨ Display the tasks.
▨ **View - Table - Work**

When you save the baseline, Project copies the Work field into the Baseline Work field.

▨ Scroll the table until you see the **% W. Comp.** column.
▨ Enter the information concerning the work actually carried out on completed tasks. If the actual work is greater than the scheduled work, enter this information into the **Actual** column: if it is less, enter the information into the **Work** column.

E-Reviewing overall project statistics

On the screen

- Project - Project Information
- Click the **Statistics** button.

In a report

- View - Reports
- Double-click **Overview** then **Project Summary**.

11.1 Communication in a project

A- Looking at communication methods

Features offered by the e-mail system

- By using an electronic mail system, workgroup members can receive, accept or refuse task assignments. They can also send and receive task updates and request or submit status reports.

- The other communication method, using **Microsoft Project Central**, offers a wider range of possibilities.

- Workgroup members can consult the tasks of all their projects, using various types of views. They can consult information on the whole project, and not only on the tasks to which they have been assigned. They can also create new tasks and send them to the project manager so that he/she can incorporate them into the project file. In some circumstances, they can also delegate tasks to other workgroup members.

- Project managers can request and receive status reports, and if necessary, consolidate individual status reports into a project status report. They can also automate project updates according to messages received from some or all members of the workgroup.

B- Looking at the different types of message

- The project manager sends a **TeamAssign** message to a workgroup member to inform him/her of a task assignment. The member can then accept or refuse this assignment.

- The project manager sends a **TeamUpdate** message to a workgroup member to inform him/her of a modification to one of his/her assigned tasks.

- The project manager sends a **TeamStatus** message to a workgroup member to request information on the progress made on a task. The member replies with information concerning the status of the task concerned. The project manager can then incorporate this information in the project plan, directly from the message.

C- Looking at message exchange processes

The message exchange process differs according to whether you use Microsoft Project Central or the e-mail system to communicate.

With e-mail

- The project manager sends messages to workgroup members from Microsoft Project 2000.

- The workgroup members reply by e-mail to the project manager's inbox.

The project manager uses his/her e-mail to view and reply to messages from the workgroup members.

With Microsoft Project Central

The project manager sends messages to workgroup members from Microsoft Project 2000.

To receive and manage these messages, the workgroup member opens a Microsoft Project Central session using a Web browser.

The workgroup member can use Microsoft Project Central to send messages to the project manager, to enter data directly into the schedule and so on.

To receive messages from workgroup members, the project manager must also open a Microsoft Project Central session. The messages are used to update the project schedule either automatically, or manually.

D-Activating a default communication method

E-mail

Tools - Options - Workgroup tab (in Project 2000)

Open the list box under **Default workgroup messages for** and choose the **Email** option.

Click the **Set as Default** button to apply this setting to all future projects. Otherwise, the message system choice will apply only to the active project.

Click **OK**.

Microsoft Project Central (Web)

Tools - Options - Workgroup tab (in Project 2000)

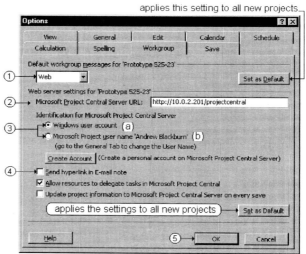

① Choose this option in the drop-down list.

② Enter the URL address of the server where Microsoft Project Central is installed.

③ To open a Microsoft Project Central session, workgroup members can use one of two authentication methods. As project manager (in agreement with the system administrator), define the authentication method you require by choosing one of the following options:

   (a)   the user will be authenticated automatically thanks to his/her Windows user account. This method offers the best security for your project files and the user does not need to enter a user name, or password to access Microsoft Project Central. Click the **Create Account** button, and confirm with the **OK** button when Project informs you that it has created your account on Microsoft Project Central. The user account is created directly in Project Central, using the user name entered when you started your computer. By default, Microsoft Project Central grants you **Manager** rights, rather than Resource or Administrator rights.

   (b)   the user will enter a user name and password to access Project Central: these will be defined in Project Central by the administrator.

④ Activate this option if you want Project to send automatic notification messages to workgroup members whenever Project Central receives new messages for them. If this is not active, workgroup members will have to check Project Central regularly for new messages.

⑤ Confirm.

⇨ *A resource may use a communication method different to that defined for the project. In this case, modify the **Workgroup** option in the **Resource Information** dialog box (use the **Project** menu) for each resource concerned.*

COMMUNICATION

E-Activating a communication method for a resource

▨ Show the **Resource Sheet** of the project concerned, select the resource you want to modify and click the ⊟ **Resource Information** tool button.

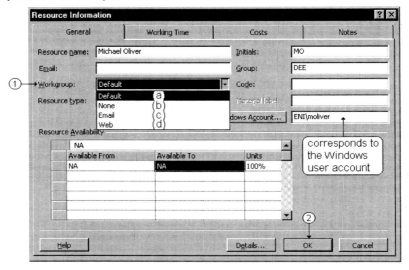

① Choose one of these options:

    (a)   to use the communication method defined by default in the project.

    (b)   if you are not using a workgroup message system in your project.

    (c)   to communicate using your company's email system.

    (d)   to communicate via Project Central.

② Confirm.

⇨ *Microsoft Project applies the* **Workgroup: Default** *option to all new Work resources that you create.*

11.2 Electronic mail

A-Entering a resource's e-mail address

▨ Show the resource sheet (**View - Resource Sheet**).

▨ Using the **Insert - Column** command, insert the **Email Address** field into the table then click **OK**.

▨ Enter the **Email Address** of each work resource with whom you want to communicate by e-mail.

⇨ *You can also enter or modify the e-mail address of a resource by selecting the resource concerned, opening the* **Resource Information** *dialog box* **(Project - Resource Information)** *and completing the* **Email** *field on the* **General** *page.*

B-Sending an e-mail to a resource

Sending a schedule note about a task

▨ In the Project 2000 application, select the task(s) for which you wish to send a comment.

The resources assigned to the selected tasks must be exclusively work resources and they must have e-mail addresses.

▨ **Tools - Workgroup - Send Schedule Note**

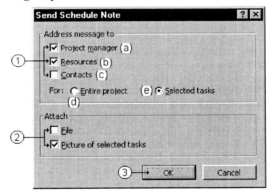

① Select the note's recipients by ticking one or more of these options:

(a)   to send the note to the project manager. In this case, the **Manager** field under the **Summary** tab of the **File - Properties** dialog box must be filled in.

(b)   to send the note to all the work resources that are assigned to all the tasks in the project (if you activate the **Entire project** option (d)) or only to the work resources assigned to the selected tasks (if you activate the **Selected tasks** option (e)).

(c)   to send your note to the contacts that the selected task(s) designate. To do this, the **Contact** field must appear in the entry sheet of the Gantt Chart and contain the name of the person in charge of this task.

② If you want to attach the whole project **File** or a **Picture of selected tasks** to your note, tick the corresponding option box(es).

③ Confirm.

Your computer's default mail application appears in a new window.

▨ Create your message using this mail program.

The *Message* window closes as soon as you have sent your message.

⇨ *Project 2000 does not indicate that you have sent a message, but your mail application stores a trace of your message in its Sent Items folder.*

⇨ *The project File sent as an attachment corresponds to the entire project file. The resource must have Project 2000 installed to open the file. The Picture of selected tasks is a bitmap image containing a copy of the selected task, for example:*

				/ '00		11 Dec '00		08 Jan '01		05 Feb 'i
ID	Task Name	Work	Baseline	F	T	S	W	S	T	M	F
9	Mechanical Design	350 hrs	350 hrs					**Andrew Blackburn**

Sending a task assignment message (TeamAssign) to a resource

▓ Select the task concerned by the assignment.

▓ **Tools - Workgroup - Team Assign**

▓ In the **Workgroup Mail** dialog box, choose the **All tasks** or **Selected task** option as required.

▓ Click **OK**.

The TeamAssign dialog box appears.

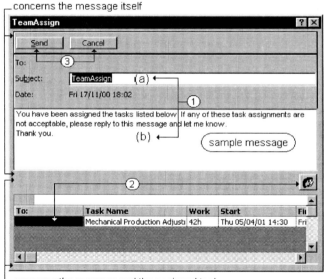

① If necessary, modify the message subject (a) and/or the message itself (b).

② Use the ▤ tool button, if necessary, to enter the resource's name in the **To** field.

③ Send the message by clicking **Send** or click **Cancel** if you decide not to send the message.

⇨ *In the Gantt Chart, the* ⬜ *icon appears to the left of the* **Task Name** *for which you sent your* **TeamAssign** *message: it stays there until all the resources have replied to refuse/accept the task.*

Sending a TeamStatus message to a resource

▨ Show the tasks then update the project (**Tools - Tracking - Update Project - OK**).

▨ Select the task concerned by the status request then use **Tools - Workgroup - TeamStatus**

▨ In the **Workgroup Mail** dialog box, choose the **All tasks** or **Selected task** option as required.

▨ Click **OK**.

The **TeamStatus** *dialog box appears.*

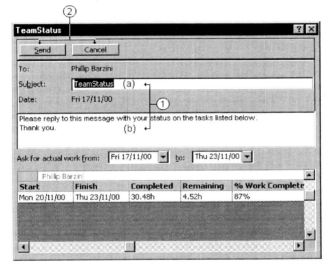

① If necessary, modify the message subject (a) and/or the message itself (b).

② Send the message by clicking **Send** or click **Cancel** if you decide not to send the message.

⇨ *In the Gantt Chart, the* ⬜ *icon is displayed to the left of the* **Task Name** *for which you sent your* **TeamStatus** *message until the resource answers your message.*

Notifying workgroup members of task modifications (TeamUpdate)

A TeamUpdate message by e-mail or via Microsoft Project Central informs resources of changes made to tasks to which they are assigned. You can send this notification message only to resources that have previously accepted the task assignment concerned by replying in the affirmative to a TeamAssign message.

As project manager, select the task concerned and make the changes you require.

*The 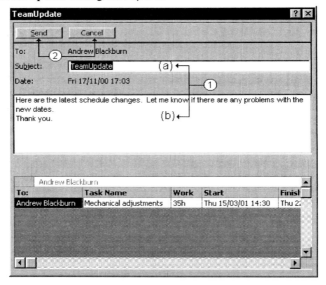 icon appears to the left of the **Task Name** for the modified task. This is to remind you to send a **TeamUpdate** message to the resources concerned.*

Tools - Workgroup - TeamUpdate

*The **TeamUpdate** dialog box opens.*

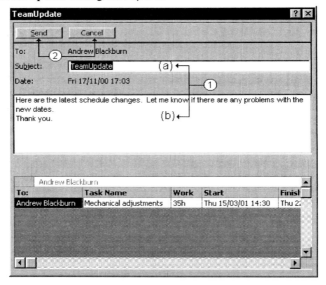

① If necessary, modify the message subject (a) and/or the message itself (b).

② Send the message by clicking **Send** or click **Cancel** if you decide not to send the message.

⇨ *The 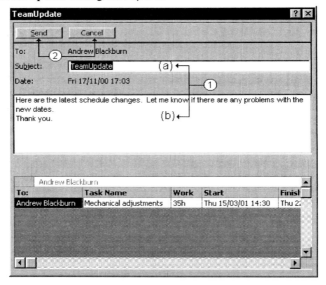 icon associated with the task disappears once the message is sent.*

⇨ *The **Update Needed** filter can display only those tasks that you have modified and for which you must send a **TeamUpdate** message to the workgroup members concerned.*

C-Replying to an e-mail with Microsoft Outlook

Accepting/refusing a task assignment (TeamAssign)

Go into Microsoft Outlook and open the **TeamAssign** message received by the resource.

Click the **Reply** button to reply to the message, or the **Close** button if you do not want to reply.

When a resource does not reply, Project considers the assignment has been accepted.

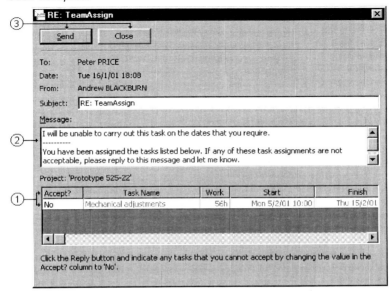

① In your reply to this message, you can accept or refuse the assignment: double-click the **Accept?** header and activate **Yes** or **No**.

② If you wish, you can add a note in the **Message** box.

③ Click **Send** or **Close**.

⇨ *If you accept a task assignment that Project 2000 has sent, Outlook 2000 will add this task into your Tasks folder.*

Providing progress status information on a task (TeamStatus)

▓ Go into Microsoft Outlook and open the **TeamStatus** message received by the resource.

▓ To postpone your reply click the **Save and Send Later** button.

▓ If you do not want to reply to the message, click **Close**.

▓ To reply to the message at once, click the **Reply** button and modify the information in the lower frame of this dialog box, if you need to. You can also add a note in the **Message** box.

▓ Click the **Send** button, to send your reply at once, or click the **Save and Send Later** button to reply later.

D-Dealing with a reply from a resource using Microsoft Outlook

When resources have replied to the messages that they received from the project manager, the project manager can update the tasks concerned from the e-mail application.

Updating task assignments with Outlook (TeamAssign)

▨ Go into Outlook, and open the message that the project manager received from the resource. The subject of the message is **RE: TeamAssign**.

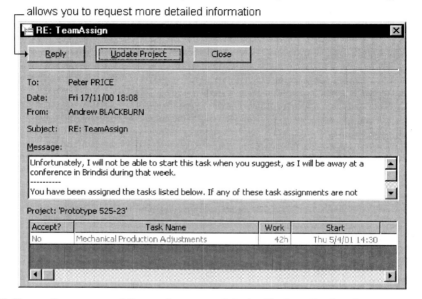

▨ To confirm or cancel the assignment, click the **Update Project** button.

If it is not already running, then Project 2000 will start up and open the project concerned automatically.

In the Entry Table of the Gantt Chart, the ⬚ *icon indicating that you are awaiting a TeamAssign reply no longer appears.*

▨ If necessary, click the ⬚ tool button in Project 2000 and modify the resource assignment to take account of the response that you received to your **TeamAssign** message.

Updating task status with Outlook (TeamStatus)

▨ Go into Outlook, and open the message that the project manager received from the resource. The subject of the message is **RE: TeamStatus**. This message is the resource's response to task status request.

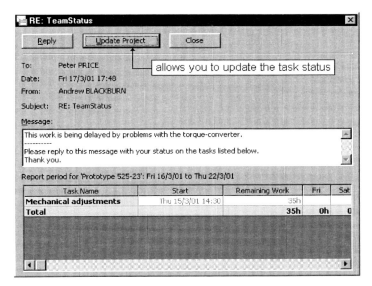

⇨ If you choose the update the project, Project 2000 will start up automatically (if it is not already running), open the appropriate project and use the transmitted data to update the corresponding fields.

⇨ In the Entry Table of the **Gantt Chart**, the 🖃 icon indicating that you are awaiting a **TeamStatus** response for the task concerned no longer appears.

11.3 Microsoft Project Central

A- Setting-up a Windows account in Project 2000

*You must have an account in order to connect to Project Central. If you chose **Windows user account** as the Microsoft Project Central identification method, then, when the project manager first sends a message to a workgroup member, Project Central automatically creates an account for the user, with **Resource** rights by default. However, to enable Project Central to do this, the project manager must first set up an account for each Workgroup member in the Project 2000 application.*

▓ Show the **Resource Sheet** and use the **Insert - Column** command to insert the **Windows User Account** field.

▓ For each resource that must connect to Project Central using his/her **Windows user account,** enter the name of this account in the following format: Domain name\User name.

⇨ *You can also define a Windows user account for a resource under the* **General** *tab of the* **Resource Information** *dialog box, by clicking the* **Windows Account** *button. Microsoft Project then searches the network for the Windows user account. If Project finds the appropriate account, then click* **Yes**. *Otherwise, if you want to choose another name, click the button to view more names.*

B-Accessing Microsoft Project Central

▒ To connect to Microsoft Project Central from Microsoft Project 2000, select the **Tools - Workgroup - TeamInbox** command.

The **Welcome to Microsoft Project Central** *page opens automatically in your browser, provided that Microsoft Project Central is able to identify your Windows user account. You must have previously defined this account on the Project Central server.*

For workgroup members who identify themselves using a Microsoft Project user name rather than a Windows user account, Project Central displays the following dialog box:

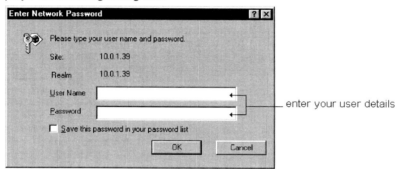

enter your user details

▒ To access Project Central from your Web browser, open your Web browser (Internet Explorer for example) and enter the URL address of your Project Central server in the address box.

C-Viewing the Microsoft Project Central screen

*This screen offers different options according to your user category (***Manager, Administrator** *or* **Resource**). *For example, as a* **Manager** *or a* **Resource**, *you will not have access the* **Admin** *page, which is reserved for* **Administrators**.

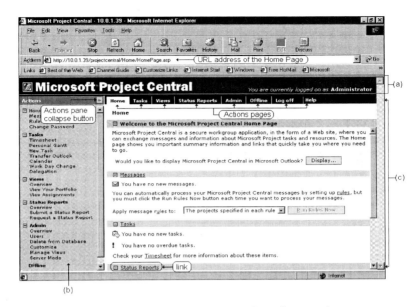

- The Microsoft Project Central screen comprises three main areas:
  - The page header (a) that indicates the name of the application (Microsoft Project Central) and your user name.
  - The Actions pane (b) that lists all the actions that you can carry out, grouped by type of action.
  - The work area (c). The menu bar at the top of the work area allows you to open the different pages of the screen. The **Home** page appears by default. The number of pages that this screen offers will vary according to your user category (**Manager, Administrator** or **Resource**).

- To access the different Actions pages, either click the corresponding tab in the work area or click the corresponding link (displayed in bold characters) in the **Actions** pane.

  In addition, the Home page provides links to other pages, such as the Tasks page.

- You can use the menu bar, either by clicking the name of the page you want to open or by pointing to the corresponding menu and then choosing one of the options that appear.

*You can access most of the Microsoft Project Central screen pages using the options in the **Actions** pane.*

D-Managing user accounts in Project Central

*Only **Administrators** can manage user accounts in Project Central. You must note that the Project Central installation program creates the **Administrator** account (with full rights) on the Project Central server automatically.*

Creating a Project Central account

▓ Point to the **Admin** menu and choose the **Users** option.

① Click this button.

② Use the vertical scroll bar to display the following entry fields:

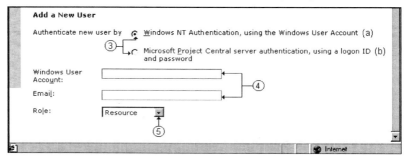

③ Choose how your new user must be authenticated, by activating one of the following options:

(a)   Choose this option if you chose **Windows user account** as the identification method in Project 2000.

(b)   Choose this option if you want the user to enter a user name and a password when he/she logs on.

④ Fill in the boxes to define the new user (these boxes will differ according to the previous option that you chose. If you chose **Windows NT Authentication** then you must specify the **Windows User Account** and an **Email** address. On the other hand, if you chose the second option, then you must specify the **User Account** and **Password** and an **Email** address.

⑤ Whatever authentication method you choose, you must choose the user's **Role** as **Resource, Manager** or **Administrator**.

Project Central provides several user categories. Attached to each category is a specific set of rights controlling access to information. When you choose the Role of the new user, you automatically assign it to the corresponding category.

You can change a user's access rights by going into the View menu and specifying the data that users from each of these categories are allowed to access. This book does not give details of how to customise views.

▓ To confirm your new user account, click the **Save Changes** button at the top of the page. Alternatively, you can cancel the account by clicking **Cancel**.

▓ If you choose to **Save Changes**, Project Central notifies you when it has completed the update. In this case, click **OK**.

Modifying a Project Central user account

▓ Click the row of the **User Account** that you want to modify and then click the **Modify User** button.

▓ Use the vertical scroll bar to display the user entry fields and make the required modifications.

▓ Click the **Save Changes** button at the top of the page to confirm your changes or click **Cancel** if you do not want to save them.

Deactivating a Project Central user account

▓ Click the row of the **User Account** that you want to delete and then click the **Delete User** button.

The following warning appears:

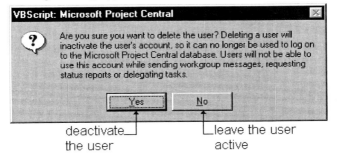

deactivate⌐   ⌐leave the user
the user   active

E- Sending a message to Project Central

*When the project manager has chosen the Web identification method and set the **Windows Account, Workgroup** and **Email** fields in the **Resource Information** dialog box for each workgroup member, he/she can send messages for these workgroup members from Project 2000 to Project Central, via the Web. The technique for sending a message via the Web is exactly the same way as the one described in the "Sending an e-mail to a resource" section.*

Sending a TeamAssign message

▦ Go into Project 2000 and display the **Gantt Chart**.

▦ Select the task concerned by the message and then use the **Tools - Workgroup - TeamAssign** command.

▦ Choose the **All tasks** option, or the **Selected task** option, as required and then click **OK**.

▦ In the **TeamAssign** dialog box, fill in the **To** field, modify the message as necessary and click **Send**.

Sending a TeamStatus message

▦ Display the **Gantt Chart**, select the task concerned then select **Tools - Workgroup - TeamStatus**.

▦ Choose the **All tasks** option or the **Selected task** option as required then click **OK**.

▦ In the **TeamStatus** dialog box, modify the message as necessary then click **Send**.

F- Using the Project Central Spooler

Project 2000 uses the Project Central spooler to forward messages from the Project 2000 workgroup to Project Central. If the message was forwarded correctly, then the Project Central Spooler displays the ▦ icon to the right of the status bar. When a problem occurs, the ▦ icon appears instead.

▦ To view a message transmission problem, double-click the ▦ icon.

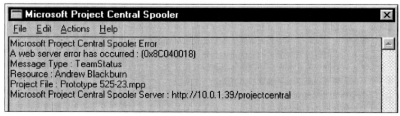

If a problem occurs with the message transmission, then the Spooler displays the type of error that occurred, the resource to whom you tried to send the message, the Project file from which you sent the message and the server that is associated with this workgroup message.

- When you have solved the problem, you can resend your message(s) using the **Actions - Resubmit Messages** command.
- To roll back all your messages, use the **Actions - Rollback Project** command.
- To close the **Spooler** window, use the **File - Exit** command.

G-Managing messages for a resource in Project Central

To view and reply to messages from the project manager, the resource must log on to Project Central.

- On the resource machine, you must go into the Web browser and enter the URL address of the server that accommodates Project Central.

*If the resource is identified by his/her Windows user account, the Microsoft Project Central Home page appears automatically. Otherwise, the resource must input his/her **User Name** and **Password** (Cf. Accessing Microsoft Project Central).*

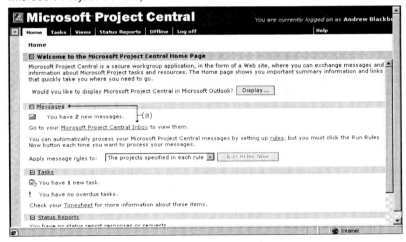

*Note that a resource cannot access the **Admin** menu. Under the **Messages** link, Project Central indicates the number of messages it has received for you (2 messages in this example).*

- In the work area of the **Home** page, click one of these links (a) to view the messages.

deletes the selected message

	From	Subject	Project	Date
selected message	Peter Price	TeamStatus	Galahad	23/11/00 16:29
	Peter Price	TeamAssign	Galahad	23/11/00 16:29

(b)

unread messages appear in bold

To open a message, select the message concerned by clicking the grey square (b) and then click the **Open Message** button.

As a workgroup member working on a project, you can receive TeamAssign messages, TeamStatus messages and TeamUpdate messages, in addition to task delegation messages that inform you of new task assignments that other resources have delegated to you.

The project manage, can receive replies to TeamAssign messages, replies to TeamStatus messages, or other messages from workgroup members that contain information that you can integrate into your project.

⇨ *You can also open a message by clicking its **Subject**.*

Accepting/refusing a task assignment (TeamAssign)

Open the **TeamAssign** message.

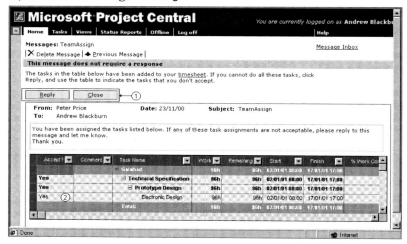

① Click the **Reply** button to reply to the message, or click the **Close** button if you do not want to reply.

② When you reply to this message, you can leave the **Yes** field under the **Accept?** header to accept the assignment, or you can click this **Yes** field and choose **No** in the drop-down list to refuse it.

If you wish, you can add a note in the **Original Message** box.

Click **Send** to send your reply or click **Close** if you want to reply later.

When you reply to a message, it disappears from the message list.

When you accept a task, it is automatically entered into the tasks list.

When the project manager reads your reply to the assignment request, he/she can update the project accordingly.

Providing progress status information on a task (TeamStatus)

Open the **TeamStatus** message.

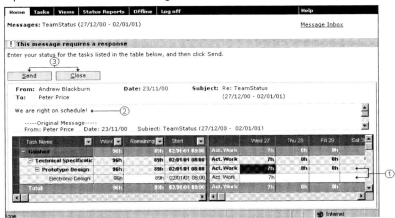

① Modify the information in the lower frame of this screen, if necessary.

② Add a note, if you wish.

③ Click **Send** to send your reply at once or click **Close** to reply later.

H-Updating tasks in Microsoft Project Central

As a Resource

As a Resource, you can use the Timesheet to work directly on the tasks that the project manager has assigned to you.

Log on to the Project Central application as a Resource.

Open the **Tasks** menu and choose the **Timesheet** option. If you are in the **Home** page, you can click the **Timesheet** link.

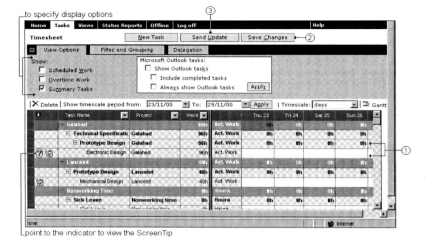

to specify display options

point to the indicator to view the ScreenTip

① To update the task progress, click in the **Act. Work** cell for the date concerned and enter the required number of hours.

② To save your changes without advising the project manager, click this button.

③ To inform the project manager of the changes that you have made to the Timesheet, click this button.

Project Central then tells you how many messages it has sent:

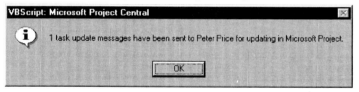

To filter or to sort the tasks that appear in the Timesheet, click the **Filter and Grouping** tab of the **Tasks** screen and specify your settings using the options and lists provided.

⇨ *The tasks are automatically grouped by Project when the messages are received.*

As project manager

When a resource either accepts or refuses a task assignment, or provides information concerning the progress that has been made with a task, the project manager must process the messages from the resource concerned to update the project.

As project manager, go into the Microsoft Project application and open the project that must be updated.

Select the **Tools - Workgroup - TeamInbox** menu option and open the **Home** page of Project Central.

- In the **Home** page, click the **Messages** link to view the list of messages that you have received.
- Click the **Task Update** subject, to open the corresponding message.

- After updating your project, Project Central asks you whether or not you wish to delete the message from your inbox.

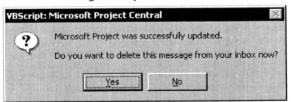

I- Delegating a task using Project Central

A workgroup member can delegate tasks to another workgroup member using the Project Central application. Before this can be done, the project manager and the Project Central administrator must apply a number of settings.

Enabling task delegation for a project

- As project manager, go into the Project 2000 application and open the project in which you want to allow task delegation. Choose the **Tools - Options** menu option, click the **Workgroup** tab and check that the **Allow resources to delegate tasks in Microsoft Project Central** option is active.
- As Administrator, log on to the Project Central application. Select the **Admin - Customize** menu option and click **Task Delegation Settings** link.

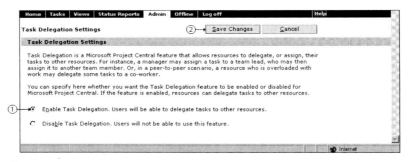

① Activate this option.

② Confirm.

Delegating a task

When the project manager and the Microsoft Project Central administrator have applied the necessary settings, a workgroup member will be able to delegate a task to another workgroup member, provided that:

- *the task is not 100% complete,*
- *the task has not already been delegated,*
- *the task does not have actual figures entered and the task is not awaiting update by the project manager.*

As the resource that would like to delegate a task, log on to Project Central and choose the **Tasks - Delegation** menu option, or open the **Delegation** page of the **Timesheet**.

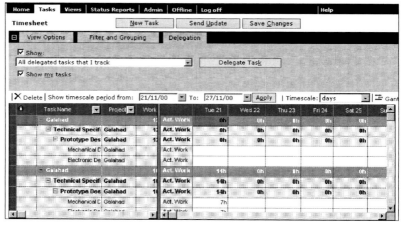

Click the task that you want to delegate to another resource and click the **Delegation Task** button.

*Project Central then starts a **Delegate task** wizard, which follows two steps.*

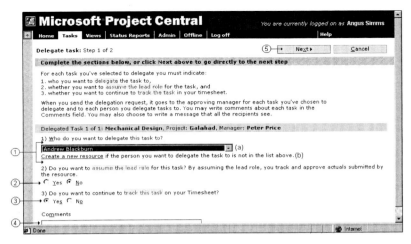

① Choose an existing resource in the drop-down list (a) or **Create a new resource** (b) if necessary.

② If you want to **assume the lead role** for this task, activate the **Yes** option in response to this question. In this case you will receive, for your approval, notification of the actual figures that the resource submits. When you have done this you must submit these updates to the project manager.

③ If you want to **track this task** after you have delegated it, activate the **Yes** option in response to this question. In this case, a copy of this task will appear in your Timesheet. You will not be able to modify it, but you will be able to track the updates that the new resource makes.

④ Enter any comments you may have.

⑤ Move on to step 2.

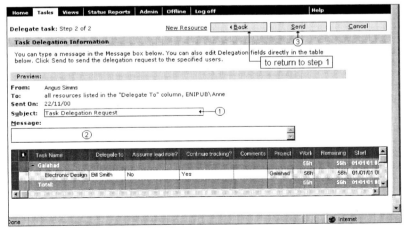

COMMUNICATION

① To modify the **Subject** of your message, select the contents of the **Subject** box and enter your new text.

② If you wish, you can enter a **Message** to accompany your delegation request.

③ To send your request to the users that the **Delegate to** column lists, click this button.

When you have sent your request, Microsoft Project Central reports back to you by confirming the names of the project manager(s) and the resource(s) to whom it has sent your request.

The project manager then receives a Task Delegation Request message stating that a resource to whom he/she assigned a task using a TeamAssign message would like to delegate this task to another resource. The project manager must read and process this message before he/she deals with any other messages that may be in his/her inbox. The project manager can choose to accept or to refuse this delegation request. If the project manager accepts the request, then the new resource assignment will replace the former resource assignment. On the other hand, if the project manager refuses the request then the assignment will remain unchanged. In this case the resource who wanted to delegate the task receives a message stating that the project manager has not accepted the request. The task is removed from task list of the resource to whom the task would have been delegated and remains only in the task list of the original resource.

⇨ *In the Tasks table the delegated tasks that you chose to track, or for which you chose to assume the lead role, appear in a different colour (in yellow). In addition, if you point to the* ▨ *icon that appears to the left of the **Task Name**, then information concerning the delegation appears as a ScreenTip.*

Shortcut keys

File

`Ctrl` N or `F1`	New	
`Ctrl` O	Open	
`Ctrl` P	Print	
`Ctrl` S	Save	

`F12`	Save As
`Ctrl` `F4`	Close
`Alt` `F4`	Exit

Edit

`Ctrl` C	Copy
`Ctrl` X	Cut
`Ctrl` V	Paste
`Del`	Delete
`Ctrl` D	Fill Down
`Ctrl` F	Find
`Ctrl` G or `F5`	Go To

`Ctrl` `F2`	Link Tasks
`Ctrl` `⇧ Shift` `F2`	Unlink Tasks
`Ctrl` Z	Undo
`Ctrl` H	Replace
`Ctrl` `Del`	Clear Contents
`Ctrl` R	Fill Right

Insert

`Inser`	New Task/New Resource	`Ctrl` K	Insert Hyperlink

Project

`⇧ Shift` `F2`	Task/Resource Information

Window

`⇧ Shift` `F11`	New Window

Planning functions

`Alt` `⇧ Shift` `→`	Promote
`Alt` `⇧ Shift` `←`	Demote
`Alt` `⇧ Shift` -	Mask subordinate tasks

`Alt` `⇧ Shift` =	View subordinate tasks
`Alt` `⇧ Shift` *	View all tasks

Opening

`Alt`	The application System menu
`⇧ Shift` `F1`	On-line help
`F10`	Menu bar
`Ctrl` `F6`	Next window

`F6`	Next sheet
`Ctrl` `⇧ Shift` `F6`	Previous window
`Alt` -	Project System menu
`F2`	Entry bar

Repeating an operation

`Ctrl` `F3`	Same filter

`Ctrl` `⇧ Shift` `F3`	Same sort

Calculating

`⇧ Shift` `F9`	The active project

`F9`	All open projects

Viewing

F3   All tasks/resources   Alt F3   **Column definition**
dialog box

Using the project window

Ctrl F10   Maximising   ⇧ Shift F11   New Windows
Ctrl F7   Moving

Restoring

⇧ Shift F3   Sort in numerical order   Ctrl F5   Project window

Timescale keys

Ctrl /   Viewing a smaller   Ctrl ⇧ Shift *   Viewing a larger timescale
timescale

Various keys

Alt F5   Go to the next   Ctrl F9   Activate/deactivate
overallocation   automatic calculation
F7   Spellcheck   Ctrl Del   Delete the contents
F1   Open Help   of a cell

Standard toolbar

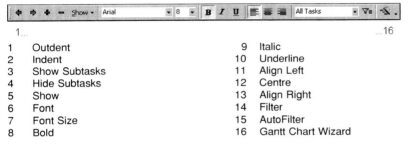

1... ...24

1	New	13	Link Tasks
2	Open	14	Unlink Tasks
3	Save	15	Split Task
4	Print	16	Task/Resource Information
5	Print Preview	17	Resource Notes
6	Spelling	18	Assign Group by Resources
7	Cut	19	Group By
8	Copy	20	Zoom In
9	Paste	21	Zoom Out
10	Format Painter	22	Go To Selected Task
11	Undo	23	Copy Picture
12	Insert Hyperlink	24	Microsoft Project Help

Formatting toolbar

1... ...16

1	Outdent	9	Italic
2	Indent	10	Underline
3	Show Subtasks	11	Align Left
4	Hide Subtasks	12	Centre
5	Show	13	Align Right
6	Font	14	Filter
7	Font Size	15	AutoFilter
8	Bold	16	Gantt Chart Wizard

Tracking Toolbar

1... ...11

1	Project Statistics	7	50% Complete
2	Update as Scheduled	8	75% Complete
3	Reschedule Work	9	100% Complete
4	Add Progress Line	10	Update Tasks
5	0% Complete	11	Workgroup Toolbar
6	25% Complete		

TOOLBARS

Web toolbar

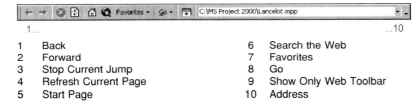

1...   ...10

1	Back	6	Search the Web
2	Forward	7	Favorites
3	Stop Current Jump	8	Go
4	Refresh Current Page	9	Show Only Web Toolbar
5	Start Page	10	Address

PERT Analysis toolbar

1...   ...7

1	Optimistic Gantt	5	PERT Entry Form
2	Expected Gantt	6	Set PERT Weights
3	Pessimistic Gantt	7	PERT Entry Sheet
4	Calculate PERT		

A

ACTIONS

B

BASELINES

C

CALENDARS

CASH FLOW

CELLS

COMMUNICATING

CONSOLIDATING

CONSTRAINTS

COPYING

COSTS

CRITICAL PATH

D

DATES

DEPENDENCIES

INDEX

R

REPORTS

RESOURCES

INDEX

INDEX